For Reference

Not to be taken from this room

WOMEN IN HISTORY

Women of the French Revolution

Thomas Streissguth

LUCENT BOOKS

An imprint of Thomson Gale, a part of The Thomson Corporation

Detroit • New York • San Francisco • San Diego • New Haven, Conn. • Waterville, Maine • London • Munich

LIBRARY OF CONGRESS CATALOGING-IN-PUBLICATION DATA

Streissguth, Thomas, 1958–
   Women of the French Revolution / by Thomas Streissguth.
       p. cm. — (Women in history)
   Includes bibliographical references and index.
   ISBN 1-59018-472-6 (hard cover : alk. paper)
   1. France—History—Revolution, 1789-1799—Women. 2. France—History—Revolution, 1789-1799—Social aspects. 3. Women revolutionaries—France—History—18th century. 4. Women in public life—France—History—18th century. I. Title. II. Series: Women in history (San Diego, Calif.)
   DC158.8.S87 2004
   944.04′082—dc22
                                                                      2004010851

Printed in the United States of America

Contents

Foreword 4

Introduction: Liberty, Equality, Sorority 6

Chapter 1:
A World Overthrown: Women of the Aristocracy 12

Chapter 2:
The Radical Urban Vanguard: Laborers
and Market Women of Paris 27

Chapter 3:
Women of the Societies 42

Chapter 4:
Women Writers 55

Chapter 5:
Peasants and Villagers 68

Chapter 6:
Women and Religion 80

Chapter 7:
Women Soldiers 92

Epilogue: Liberty and Sorority, but not Equality 104

Notes 107
Chronology 111
For Further Reading 114
Works Consulted 117
Index 122
Picture Credits 128
About the Author 128

Foreword

The story of the past as told in traditional historical writings all too often leaves the impression that if men are not the only actors in the narrative, they are assuredly the main characters. With a few notable exceptions, males were the political, military, and economic leaders in virtually every culture throughout recorded time. Since traditional historical scholarship focuses on the public arenas of government, foreign relations, and commerce, the actions and ideas of men—or at least of powerful men—are naturally at the center of conventional accounts of the past.

In the last several decades, however, many historians have abandoned their predecessors' emphasis on "great men" to explore the past "from the bottom up," a phenomenon that has had important consequences for the study of women's history. These social historians, as they are known, focus on the day-to-day experiences of the "silent majority"—those people typically omitted from conventional scholarship because they held relatively little political or economic sway within their societies. In the new social history, members of ethnic and racial minorities, factory workers, peasants, slaves, children, and women are no longer relegated to the background but are placed at the very heart of the narrative.

Around the same time social historians began broadening their research to include women and other previously neglected elements of society, the feminist movement of the late 1960s and 1970s was also bringing unprecedented attention to the female heritage. Feminists hoped that by examining women's past experiences, contemporary women could better understand why and how gender-based expectations had developed in their societies, as well as how they might reshape inherited—and typically restrictive—economic, social, and political roles in the future.

Today, some four decades after the feminist and social history movements gave new impetus to the study of women's history, there is a rich and continually growing body of work on all aspects of women's lives in the past. The Lucent Books Women in History series draws upon this abundant and diverse literature to introduce students to women's experiences within a variety of past cultures and time periods in terms of the distinct roles they filled. In their capacities as workers, activists, and artists, women exerted significant influence on important events whether they conformed to or broke from traditional roles. The Women in History titles depict extraordinary women who managed to attain positions of influence in their male-dominated societies, including such celebrated heroines as the feisty medieval queen Eleanor of Aquitaine, the brilliant propagandist of the American Revolution Mercy Otis Warren, and the courageous African American activist of the Civil War era Harriet Tubman. Included as well are the stories of the ordinary—and often overlooked—women of the past who also helped shape their societies myriad ways—moral, intellectual, and economic—without straying far from customary gender roles: the housewives and mothers, schoolteachers and church volunteers, midwives and nurses, and wartime camp followers.

In this series, readers will discover that many of these unsung women took more significant parts in the great political and social upheavals of their day than has often been recognized. In *Women of the American Revolution,* for example, students will learn how American housewives assumed a crucial role in helping the Patriots win the war against Britain. They accomplished this by planting and harvesting fields, producing and trading goods, and doing whatever else was necessary to maintain the family farm or business in the absence of their soldier husbands despite the heavy burden of housekeeping and child-care duties they already bore. By their self-sacrificing actions, competence, and ingenuity, these anonymous heroines not only kept their families alive, but kept the economy of their struggling young nation going as well during eight long years of war.

Each volume in this series contains generous commentary from the works of respected contemporary scholars, but the Women in History series particularly emphasizes quotations from primary sources such as diaries, letters, and journals whenever possible to allow the women of the past to speak for themselves. These firsthand accounts not only help students to better understand the dimensions of women's daily spheres—the work they did, the organizations they belonged to, the physical hardships they faced—but also how they viewed themselves and their actions in the light of their society's expectations for their sex.

The distinguished American historian Mary Beard once wrote that women have always been a "force in history." It is hoped that the books in this series will help students to better appreciate the vital yet often little-known ways in which women of the past have shaped their societies and cultures.

Introduction:
Liberty, Equality, Sorority

The French Revolution of 1789 changed France and the nations of Europe forever. Before the Revolution, most European states were monarchies—states ruled by a single individual with absolute sovereignty based on royal, and even divine, right. The Revolution transformed France into a republic—a state ruled by elected representatives of the people. It inspired a demand for representational government across Europe and in many other parts of the world. But the Revolution was also a social upheaval, a civil war that caused bitter, long-lasting divisions within France. It pitted the rich against the poor, the working class against the bourgeoisie (middle class), natives against foreigners, and, quite often, powerful men against the courageous and determined women who played leading roles in this violent transformation.

Women in the Old Regime

The kingdom of France under the *Ancien Regime*, or "Old Regime," was a hierarchical society. In this society an individual was born, and stayed, within a strictly defined social class. Women's roles, too, were strictly defined. Whether aristocrats, bourgeoisie, or peasants, Frenchwomen moved primarily in the private realm of hearth and family. Though some worked outside the home, nearly all were silent in the sphere of politics and in debates over public affairs. Even after reaching the age of majority (twenty-five), married women lost all legal standing on their wedding day. They were not considered full citizens. Their husbands controlled their property and had to give their permission should a wife wish to sell anything or transact any kind of business. Women had no right to sue, no right to inherit, no right to appointment in the government, no right to serve in the army, and no right to divorce. Even to bring about a legal separation from her husband, a woman had to prove that her life was in imminent danger.

Outside of marriage, Frenchwomen enjoyed a few more freedoms. Unmarried women who reached twenty-five did have the right to sign contracts in their own name. They also had the right to represent themselves in court. Widows regained the rights held by unmarried women on the death of their husbands. They also could claim their own share of the property held in common during the marriage.

The Enlightenment Reinforces Traditional Women's Roles

These legal principles were centuries old, and few women questioned them. The tradition of women as housekeepers and helpmates was ingrained in even the most radical social philosophers. The men of the influential eighteenth-century philosophical movement known as the Enlightenment, who believed that reason should replace blind religious faith, also believed that women had their place and should stay there. Jean-Jacques Rousseau, the Enlightenment philosopher whose ideas swept late-eighteenth-century France and inspired the leaders of both the American and the French revolutions, saw women's

In pre-Revolution France, the societal roles of aristocratic women like these, as well as of middle-class and peasant women, were strictly defined.

Liberty, Equality, Sorority

best hope for happiness in keeping to this traditional role. In the words of historian Marilyn Yalom:

> In the 1780s an entire nation had become captive to his vision of women as a regenerative social force issuing from their roles as devoted wives and breast-feeding mothers. Only a few dissenters . . . paused to wonder why women were so impassioned of someone who told them they were naturally inferior to men and good only for domestic servitude. . . . Rousseau's vision of the feminine was irresistible to women because it validated their desire for love and offered a new model of conjugal happiness.[1]

In his book *The Social Contract*, Rousseau also argued that society is a binding agreement between rulers and the governed. He believed that the ideal society would place actions and ideas under strict control and would direct everyone's private actions toward the common good. These notions greatly inspired the leaders of a rebellion that would unfold in 1789, completely transform France, and destroy the *Ancien Regime*.

The Estates and the Revolution

Despite the great power and prestige of France, the kingdom was in a financial mess by the 1780s. After fighting expensive wars against England in Europe and North America, the realm was bankrupt, unable to pay its debts, and unable to borrow from private lenders. The king and his court were bleeding the treasury dry with lavish entertainments, ceremonies, and other indulgences. At the same time, a complex bureaucracy was extracting a variety of duties and taxes from the citizenry, with aristocratic landowners and the clergy largely exempt. In years of poor harvests, many families went hungry, while the royal family and wealthy aristocrats lived in opulence. Poor harvest years brought hunger and sickness not only to the peasantry but also to the working people of the cities, who barely earned enough in good times to sustain their families. In the spring of 1789, the financial crisis and public discontent resulted in the convening of an assembly known as the Estates General.

The people of France looked to the Estates General as their best hope for a better future. They met at local assemblies to vote for representatives, who were divided into three "estates": The First Estate comprised the clergy, the Second Estate the nobility, and the Third Estate the rest of the population, in practice serving the interests of middle-class property owners. In notebooks known as *cahiers de doleances*, or "com-

Elected representatives of the Estates General convened in the spring of 1789 in order to address grievances against the monarchy and to propose suggestions for governmental reform.

plant books," people of all classes wrote to the king and the new assembly through the winter of 1788–1789 to express their discontent and suggest needed reforms. The cahiers revealed the many shortcomings of the monarchy and the often-corrupt bureaucracy of France, in which each individual looked out for himself and took little heed of the common good.

In one such cahier, a flower seller of Paris asked the Estates General to help enforce the rules of her guild, which had been subverted by outside profiteers:

All the unprincipled girls whom no law, no decency can restrain, throw themselves on the goods which the flower growers bring, pillage them or crush them, [and] arbitrarily set the price. . . . The petitioners ask that a police force be provided to stop large numbers of people who, claiming free trade, hang around the market every night (and especially the nights before holidays for patron saints), waiting for the flower growers and intending to abuse their good faith. They lay waste to the markets. . . . Liberty, which all orders of the State reclaim, cannot constitute an obstacle to the petitioners' request. Liberty is an enemy of license, and citizens are free so long as they obey only the laws which they impose upon themselves.[2]

The Revolution's Violent Course

The Estates General convened with high hopes in May 1789. But almost immediately, the gathering turned into a daily round of bitter argument and petty bickering. In June the members of the Third Estate broke away from the Estates General to form the National Assembly, and swore an oath to write a new constitution. In July King Louis XVI dismissed his minister of finances, Jacques Necker, over Necker's proposed radical reform of the tax system. People of all social classes looked to Necker as

On July 14, 1789, an angry mob of several thousand people stormed the royal Bastille prison in Paris, a much-hated symbol of tyranny.

Women of the French Revolution

the best hope to rescue France from total economic disaster, and his dismissal was the spark that lit a dangerous fuse of resentment and desperation. In the capital of Paris, huge mobs immediately took to the streets in protest.

On July 14, 1789, just a few days after Necker's dismissal, several thousand people stormed the royal prison known as the Bastille, a much-hated symbol of tyranny that towered above a working-class neighborhood of Paris. In August the nobles of the Second Estate nervously abolished their own aristocratic titles and privileges, bringing down the centuries-old feudal system. In October the women of Paris marched to Versailles to force the king from his palace and bring him back to the city. Over the next several years, successive assemblies broke into bitterly feuding factions while French armies fought invasion on the frontiers and mobs rioted in the capital. King Louis XVI was deposed in August 1792, imprisoned in Paris, and executed to the acclaim of an immense crowd of onlookers in January 1793. That summer, a Committee of Public Safety led by Maximilien Robespierre imposed a dic-

tatorship and embarked on the notorious Reign of Terror, in which thousands of citizens were arrested, denied the right to defend themselves, and dispatched in mass public executions.

Women at all levels of French society played important roles in the Revolution. Some found their public voice as petitioners in the public assemblies; others joined female political clubs; many joined the masses of demonstrators in the streets. The Revolution also sparked a great rise in the number of books and pamphlets written by women, many of whom called for an equal partnership with men in the struggle to establish a society based on "liberty, equality, and fraternity," the rallying cry of revolutionary France. Frenchwomen, in essence, fought for "liberty, equality, and sorority." A few women became revolutionary leaders, exposing themselves to the whirlwind unleashed by the rebellion and risking their necks for the ideals expressed in this slogan. But as the Revolution progressed, as the violence worsened and revolutionary leaders became martyrs, the women of France, like the men, found themselves simply trying to survive a terrifying social upheaval.

Chapter 1:
A World Overthrown:
Women of the Aristocracy

In 1789 the nobility of France made up a tiny percentage of the population, but they dominated French society, holding most of the wealth and land, the most powerful government posts, and the many privileges that came with their ancient feudal titles. Like many women of the bourgeoisie and working class, noblewomen found much to fault in the kingdom. Many of them felt contempt for the luxurious uselessness of the king's lavish court at Versailles. Some openly welcomed the reforms introduced by the Estates General, and some supported the establishment of a republic. By the end of the Revolution, however, these women would find their lives completely transformed. Some died at the hands of revolutionary committees and assemblies, and many more left the country as exiles. All of them faced a very uncertain future, even as the revolutionary fires died down and the country returned, fitfully, to normal.

Most aristocrats were landowners whose titles and privileges had been handed down, from one generation to the next, for centuries (although, in the eighteenth century, some members of the French nobility simply purchased their titles). While many lived in the cities, and several thousand in the capital of Paris, nearly all aristocratic families had a rural estate as well, a country home that served as a retreat in the hot summer months and as a seat of power and influence.

Although they lived at the top of the social pyramid, the women of this class led lives strictly controlled by law and custom. As girls, they had private tutors or attended a religious house, such as a convent, for their education. Their parents arranged their marriages to suitable young men—not for the sake of love but to bring some advantage, a betterment in social standing or simply property, to the family. Within an aristocratic marriage, a wife's role was to manage a household of servants, in some cases manage finances, and to continue the family line by giving birth. Noblewomen also were seen as useful interlocutors, expected to gracefully petition the authorities for jobs and favors on behalf of their husbands and male relatives.

Women of Influence

The historian Germaine de Staël was the daughter of Jacques Necker, the king's popular minister of finance. In her book *Considerations sur la Revolution Francaise*, Staël explains upper-class women's influence as intermediaries:

> Women of a certain rank were involved in everything before the revolution. Their husbands or brothers always used them to go see the ministers; they could insist without violating decorum, go too far even, without anyone's having reason to complain; all the insinuations that they knew how to make while talking, gave them a lot of influence on most of the men around.[3]
>
> Nevertheless, it was not accepted for women of the aristocracy to have political opinions or to take part in the

The French Revolution transformed the lives of the women of the nobility. While some fell victim to the judgment of revolutionary committees, many others fled the country.

governance of the country. There were no female ministers or high officials of the realm, and by the ancient Salic law, women were forbidden from ruling the country as queens. (They could serve as regents, however, if the king was underage.) Nor could women enjoy the privilege of "tax farming," in which individuals won commissions to collect taxes due in exchange for a percentage of their collections from the king's treasury.

Although they were silent on matters of politics, many aristocratic women expressed their opinions freely in their own books and diaries, and in the private forum known as the French salon, predominantly artistic gatherings hosted by upper-class women. Fired by idealism, and dissastisfied with the state of France, some of them found much to

The Salons of Revolutionary France

The French salon was a regular gathering at the home of aristocratic women, who served as hostesses to readings of poetry, performances of music, and discussions of philosophy, literature, and art. The salon hostess invited only those she thought witty and clever enough to contribute fresh ideas or amusing conversation to her gathering. Artists and writers were prized members of the salon, as these creative types often formed a cutting edge of new ideas and new styles.

The salons were places where women had their strongest effect on the arts and letters of French society. The *salonnieres* (hostesses) served as arbiters of taste and of acceptance, whether of a scientific notion or a philosophy. Writers knew that the key to their success was entrance to and patronage of a prestigious salon, where they could effectively advertise themselves and their works.

After the American Revolution, Enlightenment ideas mixed with admiration for the revolution in North America, where the rule of a distant monarch was overthrown and a new republic established. As a result, the salons took on a more political tone. Under the reign of Louis XVI, the salon became a place of political exchange in which hostesses offered a sanctuary for philosophers who saw their ideas rejected by the rigid hierarchies of the French Academy, an "official" organization of leading thinkers and writers, as well as the universities, where instruction was under control of authorities opposed to republican ideas.

cheer about in the drive for reform that preceded the French Revolution. Others, however, saw only mistakes and evil intentions. Looking back on the Revolution and the violence it brought, the aristocratic Madame de Menerville, in her book *Souvenirs d'emigration*, described Jacques Necker as follows:

> An imprudent citizen of Geneva, stuffed with arrogance, dreamed that he had the right . . . [to] improvise on the remains of our ancient monarchy. . . . He thought, in his criminal blindness, that the revolutionary flood would stop at his command as soon as he had attained his intended goal; that he could call out "That's enough!" What a fool![4]

Nevertheless, even among the aristocracy, there was a widespread feeling of dissatisfaction and restlessness under Louis XVI. At the very top, among the women of the court of Versailles, the king's lavish palace outside Paris, princesses and duchesses felt bored with routines and ceremonies and often expressed contempt for the king and the royal family. They were frustrated by the many rules of etiquette, and their daughters dreaded their formal presentation to the queen, Marie-Antoinette, an incredibly elaborate ritual that marked their arrival in society.

A Troublesome Queen

Women of years and experience saw the queen herself as an upstart foreigner who flouted tradition by defying the rules of court and of queenly behavior. The 1770 marriage of Marie-Antoinette, the fourteen-year-old daughter of the Austrian emperor Franz I and Empress Marie-Therese, had been arranged as a political alliance between France and Austria. The arrangement brought peace, temporarily, to the two nations, but it also led to suspicion of Marie-Antoinette by aristocrats and the common people. For years before the Revolution, pamphleteers had criticized and ridiculed her, and many believed she was an Austrian spy.

Marie-Antoinette also troubled members of the court with her disdain of etiquette and tradition. She grew very bored with the court's strict rules of behavior (such as bowing her head at the entrance of a mere duchess and pressing down against the arms of her chair, as if to rise, for a princess of the royal family). She was exasperated by the elaborate morning rituals of washing and getting dressed, which involved several ladies-in-waiting who followed strict rules on how to help the queen into her clothes, one item at a time. Even the simple act of drinking a glass of water demanded a certain procedure; if a lady-in-waiting or "first lady of the

Many noblewomen disliked Marie-Antoinette (pictured). They were scandalized by her disdain for etiquette, and some even suspected her of spying for Austria.

bedchamber" was not present to hand her the glass, the queen's thirst went unquenched.

Marie-Antoinette set about breaking many of these rules personally. She allowed herself to be seen in public in the company of men—a shocking new sight for the courtiers of Versailles. For the first time in centuries, a queen of France also allowed male servants to wait on her. The queen invited all sorts of actors, artists, musicians, and other members of the lower classes to Versailles to perform or simply to mingle at court—another bold defiance of tradition.

One man, the Prince de Montbarey, who served Louis as the secretary of state, did not look favorably on these actions:

> The Queen's youth and her craving for pleasure led her to find the rules of etiquette too troublesome, and she regarded those who still held to them as silly creatures who must be got rid of. This Princess, who otherwise had so many rare qualities and whose only defects were those of her years, did not remark, or allow herself to be told, that at court appearances are more important than reality.[5]

For many people in France, Marie-Antoinette came to represent all that was wrong with the French monarchy. She became the focus of popular resentment and the target of scurrilous, pornographic pamphlets ridiculing her appearance and accusing her of treason, espionage, and immorality. On October 5, 1789, these resentments coalesced at the gates of Versailles in the form of an unruly mob of several thousand women, who had marched fourteen kilometers from the center of Paris to demand bread. That night, a small crowd of women rushed the queen's apartments and got as far as the antechamber of her bedroom. They killed two guards standing at the doorway but retreated before reaching the queen. The next day, Marie-Antoinette appeared on a balcony to quiet the mob. The royal family then proceeded under guard to the palace of the Tuileries where they came under close watch by the citizens of Paris.

Favoring the Revolution

By this time, those who lived permanently at Versailles saw mockery of the court as fashionable. A lady-in-waiting of Versailles, Henriette-Lucy Dillon, marquise de La Tour du Pin, described the boredom and dissolution in her *Memoirs*:

The profligate reign of Louis XV had corrupted the nobility and among the Court Nobles could be found instances of every form of vice. Gaming, debauchery, immorality, irreligion, all were flaunted openly. . . . The rot started at the top and spread downwards. Virtue in men and good conduct in women became the object of ridicule and were considered provincial. . . . The Revolution of 1789 was only the inevitable consequence and, I might almost say, the just punishment of the vices of the upper classes.[6]

In the streets and among the working people of France, this fashionable mockery was echoed in a sullen, menacing anger toward the king, his queen, and their many useless courtiers. The widespread discontent caught up many aristocratic women in the patriotic fervor of the first year of the Revolution, when people of all social classes optimistically saw the Estates General, the representative assembly called by Louis XVI, as a hopeful sign of peaceful reform and self-renewal. Optimism for the future, among all ranks of men and women, reached its high point on July 14, 1790, the first anniversary of the fall of the Bastille prison, a symbol of tyranny and arbitrary authority. The demolition of the Bastille was commemorated by a Festival of the Federation on the

Champ de Mars, a field lying just outside the city of Paris. As described by Madame de Tourzel, even women from the highest social class enthusiastically took part in the festivities:

> Everyone wanted to have a part of the action. . . . Even the ladies had themselves driven there in carriages so they could help fill the wheelbarrows; and everyone who might have passed quietly by the Champ-de-Mars without stopping ran the risk of being insulted. . . . There were workers, bourgeois men and women, Carthusian monks and others from different orders, military men, beautiful ladies, men and women from every class and all stations of society. . . . Several of them, even from the highest social class, became so fatigued that they fell sick, and finished by being victims of their patriotic zeal.[7]

All over France, in the meantime, patriotic zeal was turning into bloodshed. Aristocratic families saw their houses seized and burned. Peasants and townspeople turned these noble families out into the streets to be mocked and assaulted. As the Revolution turned chaotic, the badges of aristocracy—fine clothes, servants, and elaborate carriages—grew unfashionable and downright dangerous.

The charge of "aristocrat" was equated with treason and became punishable by death. Thousands of noble families fled the country to become émigrés, an action that brought seizure of their property and a warrant for their arrest and execution should they ever return. Their inclusion on the official list of émigrés condemned thousands of aristocrats to years of wandering in foreign countries, and, for some, permanent exile elsewhere in Europe and in North America. The émigrés knew, however, that wandering and homesickness were far preferable to the bloody end suffered by many French noblewomen, including the queen herself.

Days of Terror

The last governess of the king's children, Louise Elizabeth de Tourzel, had accompanied the royal family in its forced journey to Paris in October 1789. There she saw the king, queen, and their son and daughter reduced to virtual prisoners, forced by the crowd to appear before them wearing the cockade, a ribbon of blue, white, and red that had become a popular symbol of the Revolution. On the night of June 20, 1791, the king decided to flee Paris and make a run for the eastern frontier of France, where he and his family would cross into safe territory controlled by Austria. Louis disguised himself by dressing as Madame de

As the Revolution turned chaotic, mobs of revolutionaries like these stormed the homes of the nobility, seized and destroyed their property, and even assaulted the aristocrats themselves.

Tourzel's own valet, while Marie-Antoinette took on the guise of Madame de Tourzel's chambermaid. About halfway to the border and safety, the royal carriage reached the town of Varennes, where the king was recognized by a postmaster. The coach was turned back, and the royal family suffered a humiliating procession back to the capital and house arrest in the Tuileries, where the people greeted them with stony silence. The monarchy was doomed; from that time on, the people and the Revolution turned against the king.

On August 10, 1792, a huge mob invaded the grounds of the Tuileries palace. Thousands of sansculottes (the city's working classes) swarmed into the palace, running amok through the gilded halls and killing hundreds of Swiss guards, while the royal family and their ladies-in-waiting desperately tried to escape. One man grabbed Madame Jeanne-Louise Campan, the first lady-in-waiting to the queen, and raised his dagger, poised to murder her. Madame Campan described the moment in her memoirs:

Intellect and Intuition

❧

Despite their comforts and privileges, many aristocratic women shared the excitement over the convening of the Estates General at Versailles in May 1789. As did the men of their class, they saw the Estates as a golden opportunity for the nation to correct past injustices. The Estates had not convened since 1614; the grand procession of representatives in Paris that took place on May 5 showed that something new and exciting was definitely afoot. Germaine de Staël, the daughter of Jacques Necker, welcomed the grand procession of representatives in May 1789 with feelings of hope and enthusiasm. An acclaimed *salonniere* and skilled writer, Staël was accompanied by a friend who had a very different perception, as Staël later described in "The Opening of the Estates General May 1789," an essay collected in *Considerations sur la Revolution Francaise*:

I had found a place by the window next to Mme. de Montmorin, wife of the Minister of Foreign Affairs. At the sight of these representatives of the whole nation, assembled for the first time in France, I must confess I abandoned myself to some very lively hopes. Mme. de Montmorin was a woman of no intellectual distinction whatsoever, but the determination in her voice made some effect on me. "You are wrong to celebrate," she said. "Great disasters will come of this—disasters for France, disasters for ourselves." This unhappy woman died on the scaffold, along with one of her sons. The other son drowned; her husband was killed in the massacre on September 2 of that year; her older daughter died in a prison hospital; and her younger daughter, Mme. de Beaumont, an intelligent, generous woman, was crushed by her sorrow before she reached the age of thirty.

I was on my knees, my executioner released me and said "Get up, you slut, the nation's letting you off." The coarseness of those words did not prevent me from suddenly experiencing an indescribable feeling which came almost as much from love of life as from the idea that I was going to see my son again and everything that was dear to me. . . . One rarely sees death so closely without experiencing it.[8]

The royal family was removed to the

Temple Prison, where they were kept as prisoners of the revolutionary government. Marie-Antoinette was allowed some comforts there, including several ladies-in-waiting, and the company of a close friend, the Princess Marie-Therese de Lamballe. On August 19, however, the princess was carried off to the Prison de la Force, a prison reserved mainly for prostitutes, by a mob.

On September 2, news of the advance of the armies of Austria and Prussia into French territory reached Paris.

The news inspired rumors that a conspiracy against the Revolution was afoot in the capital. The result was a massacre in the prisons of Paris; gangs of men armed with muskets and pikes invaded the prisons and murdered thousands of helpless men, women, and children in their cells. On September 3, a mob arrived at the Prison de la Force, dragged the Princess de Lamballe to a hastily convened court, and brought her out to the prison courtyard, where she was torn to pieces after refusing to take

Revolutionaries force King Louis XVI and the royal family to return to Paris after their unsuccessful attempt to flee the country on June 20, 1791.

A World Overthrown: Women of the Aristocracy

an oath denouncing the monarchy. The mob cut off her head, stuck it on a pike, carried it to the Temple, and paraded it before Marie-Antoinette's window to taunt the queen.

A stranger saved Madame de Tourzel from a similar fate. A sympathetic man, known to her as Monsieur Hardy, passed out generous portions of wine to the mob gathered in the courtyard. With her captors softened up, Madame de Tourzel was acquitted by her court after a short interrogation. She was brought to the door of the prison where, much to her surprise, the mob waiting outside hailed her and then conducted her and her daughter in a coach through the streets of Paris. Unlike the Princess de Lamballe, the queen, and many other aristocratic women, Madame de Tourzel would survive the Revolution.

A Death at Aristocratic Hands

Not all nobles enjoyed comfort, property, and feudal privileges. Many of them possessed only their titles, living in -squalid country homes with no servants and very little furniture or property of any kind. Their poverty was exacerbated by the tradition that dictated they could not soil their hands by manual labor or by running a business. One such fallen noble family were the Cordays of Normandy. They had been members of the highest military caste, known as the "nobility of the sword," since the eleventh century. By the time of Louis XVI, however, they lived in a small cottage among the peasants. According to historian Stanley Loomis:

> For nearly five centuries the purest Norman blood had flowed in the Cordays' veins. . . . They bred with the indifference of their livestock, and their once extensive property, though protected by the laws of primogeniture [inheritance by eldest son], had been divided and subdivided many times. . . . In many of these houses the countess would breed her children beneath a roof shared by the rutting hogs and cattle of her husband's barnyard. . . . The count or marquis wore wooden shoes like his peasants and dressed little better than they.[9]

Despair at the poverty of her family fired Charlotte Corday with enthusiasm for the Revolution. Corday supported the Girondin party of deputies (named for the Gironde region of southwestern France), who favored a constitutional monarchy such as the one in England. In June 1793, however, Charlotte Corday saw the radical Jacobin faction, with the help of the Parisian sanscullotes, evict the Girondins from the National Convention, the legislature that had succeeded the National Assembly. Many of the Girondin deputies were condemned to imprisonment and death on the guillotine, while the radical firebrand Jean-Paul Marat egged on the mobs and the revolutionary tribunals. In his newspaper, *L'Ami du Peuple*, Marat incited the people to acts of mob violence against the royalists and aristocrats as well as moderates such as the Girondins.

When she heard of the fall of the Girondins, Corday formed a bitter hatred for Marat. She began to plot his death, seeing it as a way for the Revolution to regain its ideals and cure itself of the mindless violence inspired by Marat's newspaper. A devoted reader of ancient history and the biographies of the Greek writer Plutarch, she also fancied herself in the role of Brutus, Julius Caesar's assassin, whose knife struck a fatal blow against tyranny. In early July 1793, she left her family and friends in Normandy and traveled by coach, alone, to Paris. There she took a hotel room, called on Girondin deputies from Normandy, and bought a wood-handled, five-inch kitchen knife at a cutler's shop.

On July 13, with the knife hidden in the folds of her dress, Corday arrived at the apartment of Jean-Paul Marat. At the door, she found Marat's common-law wife, Simonne Evrard, barring the way. Corday called out to Marat, declaring that she knew the names of traitors to the Revolution in Normandy. Intrigued by the chance to send more victims to the guillotine, Marat told Evrard to allow her to pass. Corday entered the apartment to find her prey soaking in a large bath, where he spent many hours

Charlotte Corday murdered the radical Jean-Paul Marat in July 1793.

Charlotte Corday is led to the guillotine. Corday was executed just days after she murdered Marat.

every day writing letters and newspaper articles and trying to ease a painful skin disease. Within a few minutes, Corday had pulled the knife from her dress and plunged it into Marat's chest. While Marat screamed in agony, Corday fled the room, only to be stopped and arrested before reaching the front door.

For the assassination of Marat, Charlotte Corday was quickly imprisoned,

Women of the French Revolution

tried, and executed. While in prison, she wrote a letter of apology and explanation to her father: "Forgive me, dear Papa, for having disposed of my life without your permission. I have avenged many innocent victims and I have prevented many future disasters. The people will one day be disabused and be glad to have been delivered of a tyrant."[10] In another letter, this one to the radical deputy Charles Babaroux, Corday explained her actions this way:

> I have never hated a single human being. . . . And I pray that those who regret my passing to consider that one day they will rejoice to see me enjoy the repose of the Elysian Fields with Brutus and the ancients. For the moderns, there are so few patriots who know how to die for their country; everything is egoism; what a sorry people to found a Republic.[11]

For many, Corday symbolized the futile resistance of the fallen nobility to an inevitable tide that was sweeping their entire class into oblivion. Although she saw her action as a heroic effort to destroy the worst elements of the Revolution and put it back on the right path, her murder of Marat had the effect of spreading fear and paranoia among the radical deputies and the sansculottes, the poor and working-class Parisians who now controlled the streets of the capital. This fear would help inspire the Reign of Terror of 1793–1794, when Jacobin leaders such as Maximilien Robespierre would order the show trials and mass beheadings of thousands of suspected aristocrats, moderates, and other presumed opponents of the Revolution.

The Fate of Marie-Antoinette

On January 21, 1973, Louis XVI was executed on the guillotine. His queen and children languished in the Temple until August, when Marie-Antoinette and her daughter were moved to the Conciergie prison—her son had been taken from her in July. In September her daughter too was removed from her, and in October the queen, now called the Widow Capet, was subjected to a humiliating two-day trial whose outcome was never in doubt.

On October 16, thirty-seven-year-old Queen Marie-Antoinette followed Charlotte Corday and hundreds of other aristocratic women to the guillotine. On their ride to the scaffold in the large wooden carts known as tumbrels, the prisoners were mocked by the crowds and by the *insulteuses*, women hired by the revolutionary Commune (city government) of Paris to whip the crowds into a frenzy by hurling insults at those condemned to death. Leading the applause of the crowds at the foot of the guillotine

The Queen Goes to the Scaffold

❦

Marie-Antoinette went to the guillotine on October 16, 1793. Crowds of citizens lined the streets of Paris to watch the queen, her hair shorn, dressed in a simple white frock, ride in her tumbrel to the scaffold. Quoted in Cobb and Jones, *Voices of the French Revolution*, an English witness, Helen Maria Williams, recalled the queen's final moments:

> On her way to execution, where she was taken after the accustomed manner in a cart, with her hands tied behind her, she paid little attention to the priest who attended her. She reached the place of execution about noon, and when she turned her eyes towards the [Tuileries] palace, she became visibly agitated. She ascended the scaffold with precipitation, and her head was in a moment held up to the people by the executioner.

Guards arrive to escort Queen Marie-Antoinette to the guillotine in 1793.

The execution of Marie-Antoinette became one of the most famous events of the French Revolution, rivaling the fall of the Bastille and the execution of King Louis XVI. While the frivolity and wealth of the queen symbolized a corrupt aristocracy, her bloody end represented the violent excess of the Revolution, in which thousands died, were imprisoned, or were driven out of the country for their social status or their political views.

were women known as *tricoteuses*, or "knitters," who calmly went about their knitting while heads rolled and blood splashed down on the cobblestones. The *insulteuses and tricoteuses* were the sworn enemies of the aristocrats. They represented the leading female edge of the Revolution, the company of radical city women who embodied the passion of the lower classes for justice and vengeance.

Chapter 2:
The Radical Urban Vanguard: Laborers and Market Women of Paris

Paris, the capital and largest city of France, was the epicenter of the French Revolution. In Paris, revolutionary governments rose and fell, new constitutions were written, crowds of people rioted and brawled in the streets, and the king was imprisoned and finally put to death. The Revolution of Paris, in turn, was driven in large part by the city's women. The militant women of Paris formed an important revolutionary vanguard, fighting in the front ranks for an end to a system they saw as corrupt and unjust.

In 1789 women made up the majority of the population in Paris. Many women had migrated to the city from the countryside, where employment was scarce and hunger was common. They found meager jobs to earn a living and enjoyed few legal rights. Nevertheless, Parisian women exerted a very strong influence over the social life of city neighborhoods. This power, in turn, galvanized the popular revolution in the streets. In his book *The Making of Revolutionary Paris*, historian David Garrioch explains:

> Despite women's inferior economic and legal position, they exerted considerable power through their role as neighborhood opinion makers and commentators. The street, and particularly the markets, were in a sense female territory. . . . Most stallkeepers were women and they knew more about neighborhood affairs than anyone else. The women in the street—including those who brought their work downstairs to sit with neighbors outside the house—kept an eye on what was going on and were often the first to intervene in quarrels.[12]

The women of the city took on all sorts of occupations to earn an independent living or to supplement their husbands' income. Women were a majority of the workforce in the textile factories that produced clothing, carpets, and finished cloth. Others worked in typographers' shops, skilled in engraving and the casting of type, which required a small and steady hand. Females also made up the majority of domestic servants at the time of the Revolution. Thousands of women worked as peddlers, selling fruit, vegetables, articles of clothing, and other goods on street corners and in public squares. Laundresses, who worked together in large and unruly groups along the banks of the Seine River, were notorious for their rowdiness. But the most familiar group of working women

to the residents of Paris were the market women and *poissardes* (fishwives) who worked in Les Halles, the city's vast central marketplace.

For centuries, market women had taken part in an annual ritual, an appearance before the king and queen to pay their respects and ritual tribute. They brought produce, flowers, and other gifts, symbols of their bounty and their role as providers, and in return received the king's blessing. But in the later years of the eighteenth century, when the price of bread was rising and hunger was overtaking much of the population, these ceremonies

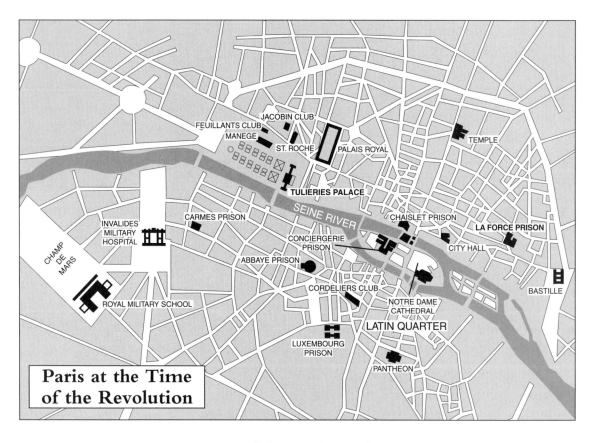

Paris at the Time of the Revolution

Women of the French Revolution

turned into angry encounters. In July 1789, when the workers of Paris marched on the Bastille prison, a symbol of royal tyranny, female workers and market women appeared at the front of the crowds that gathered before the prison gates. On October 5, the working women of Paris gathered for an extraordinary march to the palace of Versailles, the symbol of the ancient French monarchy and the home of King Louis XVI.

The March to Versailles

Early on that fateful morning, a young woman walked through the alleys of the Chatelet quarter of Paris. She was beating a drum and complaining loudly to all who would listen about the high price of bread. The drum, and the ringing of a bell at the Church of Sainte Marguerite, was a summons and a call to arms. Several thousand women and fishwives of Les Halles and the Faubourg Saint-Antoine, a neighborhood of laborers and artisans, gathered before the Hotel de Ville, the city hall of Paris. A newspaper

On October 5, 1789, a crowd gathers outside the Hotel de Ville in Paris as a group of working women ransacks the building for weapons.

editor, Elysee Loustalot, described the astonishing scene to his readers:

Women of the people, principally merchants from the central markets and workers from the Faubourg Saint-Antoine, took upon themselves the *"salut de la patrie"* [the nation's condition]. They rounded up in the streets all the women they encountered there; they even went into houses to lead off all those who could add to the numbers in the procession; they went to the square in front of the Hotel de Ville.[13]

The women burst in to the Hotel de Ville. While the city's officials and police looked on, they ransacked the building and gathered hundreds of muskets and two cannons. They angrily denounced and threatened the mayor of Paris and the Marquis de Lafayette, the commander of the National Guard. In a heavy rainstorm, they marched west, forcing more female passersby into their company, toward the king's palace at Versailles, fourteen kilometers from the Hotel de Ville.

At the town of Versailles, writes historian Simon Schama, they encountered an extraordinary sight:

Sporting a plumed hat and a blood-red riding coat and carrying pistols and a saber, this was Theroigne de Mericourt, whose appearance was obviously designed to attract attention and on whom nineteenth-century writers developed a fixation as an "Amazon" of the Revolution. . . . Though Theroigne was, by all reliable accounts, strikingly beautiful, she was important on the fifth of October only for her appearance as a symbol of the Revolution as an omnipotent woman.[14]

When they reached the sprawling palace, the leaders of the crowd broke in to the meeting hall of the National Assembly, the new legislature of the Third Estate. The women took their places in the Assembly seats, and one of them sat in the president's chair. They shouted and declaimed their own views and mocked the legislators—all of them members of the middle class, and all of them men—by passing their own new laws by acclamation. They demanded that the king accept the Declaration of the Rights of Man and of the Citizen, a document he had refused to endorse, and sign a decree abolishing the privileges of the aristocracy. Both documents had been passed by the Assembly but rejected by the king, who sought to keep the monarchy's authority over the actions of elected representatives.

The king, rattled by this invasion of his palace sanctuary, sent a message to the Assembly hall, promising that Paris would be provided with bread. In the evening, with the noisy and hungry crowd growing unruly in the courtyards and hallways of Versailles, he also accepted the decrees. The market women, however, were not placated. Through the night, they confronted and attacked the

Sympathy for the March on Versailles

When it comes to the care and feeding of a family, women of all social classes could feel a common cause and concern. Although she was a celebrated novelist and a member of the upper class, the writer Elisabeth Geunard shows empathy for the women marching on Versailles in October 1789, as quoted by Marilyn Yalom in *Blood Sisters*:

> You have to be a mother and have heard your children ask for bread you cannot give them to know the level of despair to which this misfortune can bring you . . . With children who are hungry and ask repeatedly and tearfully for food—it seems as if each sound issuing from their chests parched by poverty is the point of a dagger striking their mother's heart. She cannot bear it, and her pain makes her capable of doing anything because she sees nothing, feels nothing, except the imperious law of nature commanding her not to let those perish who owe her their birth.

Armed with farm implements and weapons seized from the Hotel de Ville, women and children march toward Versailles.

royal bodyguards as the king and his queen, Marie-Antoinette of Austria, cowered in their sumptuous rooms. The next day the women of Paris forced the king and his family, as well as the National Assembly, to return to the Tuileries palace in Paris, to work and live among the people.

A Fusillade on the Champ de Mars

For the next two years, working-class women of Paris occupied the front lines of the Revolution. They marched and demonstrated, confronted the king's guards at the Tuileries, and assassinated royalists and suspected counterrevolutionaries in the streets. Their militancy posed a dilemma for male revolutionary leaders, who sought to harness their energy but who still could not accept women outside of their traditional roles as domestic providers and housekeepers.

The Constitution of 1791 inspired another confrontation between Parisian

The revolutionaries storm the National Assembly hall at Versailles. There, they demanded that the king sign a decree abolishing the privileges of the aristocracy.

Women of the French Revolution

women and the king. The constitution established a new voting system based on a poll tax. "Active" citizens were defined as those who paid at least three days of work as tax, which gave them the right to vote. "Passive" citizens did not enjoy this right. All women were considered passive citizens and still had no right to bear arms, to vote, or to stand for election.

On July 17, a crowd of "passive" Parisians gathered to sign a petition against the constitution on the Champ de Mars, while a detachment of the National Guard under the Marquis de Lafayette faced the petitioners. When the crowd taunted and threatened the guardsmen, Lafayette gave the order to disperse them. The guard opened fire, killing fifty people.

The massacre on the Champ de Mars threw the city into a frenzy of anger and inspired rebellion among many of Lafayette's own troops. Through the fall and winter of 1791, radical revolutionary leaders, who advocated all-out war against the aristocracy and those sympathetic to the king, took control of events. These radicals called the people to action against the counterrevolutionaries in their newspapers and pamphlets, one of which, *Les lettres bougrement patriotiques de la Mere Duchesne*, captured the rough voice and vulgarity of a revolutionary Frenchwoman:

There's something to talk about, d—it. In the old days when we wanted to speak out, we were made to shut our mouths and told politely that we reasoned like animals—a bit like f—animals. F—me! it's all different now, we women have got important since the Revolution. By God! freedom has given us wings! Today we fly like eagles! I may be ignorant and uneducated, but I can still hold my own in politics.[15]

Storming the Tuileries

Since the storming of the Bastille, Paris had been rocked by riots over the rising price and scarcity of basic commodities. Women stormed the city's grocery shops, seized staple goods, including sugar, and sold them for what they considered a fair price. The "sugar riots" inspired a violent response from the city's merchants—not against the female rioters but against the hoarders whom everyone suspected of cheating the people for the sake of profit. At the Assembly on January 26, 1792, one of these merchants proclaimed:

The citizens of the Faubourg St-Antoine leave it to the women, the elderly and the children to shout for sugar. The men of 14 July do not fight for bonbons. Our wild and savage nature responds only to liberty

A peasant mob storms the Tuileries palace in August 1792. Many women were active participants in the attack.

and the sword. Let the conspirators, the hoarders, the enemies of order know that while their hired brigands are inciting the people to attacks on property, we are calmly forging the pikes which will exterminate them, the scoundrels! So let those who disturb the peace tremble: the people's patience is wearing thin![16]

The sugar riots continued in February, as historian George Rude describes:

The disturbance began in the Beaubourg section in the city centre on 20 January with a riot of market women. . . . On the 14th [of February], over twenty grocers in the Rue du Faubourg alone were threatened

Women of the French Revolution

with invasion, and several were forced to sell sugar at 20 sous a pound before order could be restored. . . . The next day, women—nearly always on such occasions in the forefront—rang the bell in the church of St. Marcel, and attempts were made to force the warehouse doors.[17]

After the royal family was caught trying to flee France in June 1791, the public lost all faith and confidence in their king. The mobs of Paris suspected Louis of conspiring with Austria against the French army in order to regain his authority in France. They suspected his queen, the foreigner Marie-Antoinette, of being an Austrian spy and of urging Louis to fight the decrees and laws passed by the legislature. On the night of August 10, 1792, armed mobs marched on the Tuileries palace. One eyewitness described the attack:

I saw, an instant before the combat, an amiable and still young lady with a saber in her hand, standing on a rock, and I heard her harangue the multitude. Suddenly, thousands of women hurled themselves into the fray, some with sabers, others with pikes; I saw several kill Swiss guards there. Other women encouraged their husbands, their children, their fathers.[18]

During the next month, the advance of counterrevolutionary armies on the eastern frontier inspired an orgy of bloodshed in the panicked city. Thousands of people were cut down in the streets, monasteries, hospitals, and prisons of the city. In a letter to her husband, a housewife described the scene:

Listen and tremble: the alarm cannon booms around midday, the tocsin rings, the call to arms sounds out. People come and go in the streets. Everything has been in a state of acute crisis; the municipality's moving proclamations attracted the people's attention and touched their hearts:"Fly to the aid of your brothers! To arms! To arms!" Everyone is running and hurrying around. Forty thousand men are leaving tonight to descend on the Prussians, whether at Verdun or before, if the enemy are advancing.[19]

The War of the Cockades

In the charged atmosphere of revolutionary Paris, small matters of dress and deportment took on political meaning. One important symbol of the committed revolutionary was a small cockade, a ribbon in "tricolor," or blue, white, and red. On April 3, 1793, the Convention passed a decree that stated that all citizens must wear them. The cockade appeared on

Marianne

In their paintings, sculptures, and engravings, the artists of revolutionary France used women as symbols of the fight against tyranny and monarchy. Armed with pistols or a saber and wearing the red "liberty cap," women were shown at the head of the common people, boldly urging them on to acts of courage and defiance. Out of these works emerged a national symbol, christened Marianne, that came to stand for the new republic and its ideals. According to some historians, Marianne first appeared in October 1792 in southern France. Making the rounds at that time was a song by Guillaume Levabre called "La Guerison de Marianne." The song, and the legend of a young woman who helped sick and wounded revolutionary fighters, introduced the symbolic Marianne to all parts of France.

In modern times, Marianne has endured and thrived. She appears on stamps, coins and banknotes, official documents, and the official seal of the French Republic. Every few years, the government selects a new Frenchwoman as a model for Marianne. She has taken on the image of famous film stars such as Brigitte Bardot and Catherine Deneuve and models such as Ines de la Fressange and Laeticia Casta, the current Mariannes.

Marianne, an enduring symbol of the fight against tyranny, leads the people into battle.

Women of the French Revolution

hats, coats, and dresses; those whose sympathies lay elsewhere wore them to comply with the law but, in defiance, hid them underneath lapels and in the folds of dresses.

The decree did not refer to women, an ambiguity that led to the "War of the Cockades" in the late summer. By this time, market women were blaming the Convention for the chaos that was reigning in the streets. They denounced the police surveillance of prices and goods in the marketplaces, which they believed was hurting their business. Many of them refused to wear the cockade, a practice that brought insults, confrontations, and fights. In Les Halles, the market women's domain, they often refused goods to women wearing the cockades. They boldly tore the ribbons and the red "liberty caps" from their victims, sometimes threatening them and chasing them out of the neighborhood.

Hearing of these incidents, the Convention passed a new law on September 21 decreeing that any woman seen not wearing a cockade would serve eight days in prison. Those who assaulted others for wearing the cockade, or who defaced or insulted it in any way, would serve six years.

The market women complied with the new law, and for a while the situation calmed. But their resentment of this defeat smoldered underneath their grudging compliance. Many women working in public saw female militancy as a prime cause of their problems: food shortages, arbitrary laws, and constant turmoil. They also feared that the Convention would decree more laws, such as the compulsory wearing of the liberty cap, compulsory military service, compulsory voting, compulsory bearing of arms, and compulsory cutting of hair short to conform to the revolutionary ideal of "republican" appearance.

The market women found a crucial ally in the Jacobins, the radical faction that was now in control of the Convention. Although the Jacobin men had once welcomed the support of female political clubs, such as the Society of Revolutionary Republican Women, their opinion of female activism was changing. The insistent and constant petitions, the interruptions in the club meetings and the legislature, the agitation over the cockades, and the constant demands for the right to vote and to bear arms rankled many of them. With the support of the market women, the Jacobins went on the attack.

They found their opportunity in October, when the market women demanded an end to female political societies. The petitioners found a sympathetic hearing. Andre Amar, the head of a committee investigating the brawls in the marketplace, proclaimed:

The tri-color cockade, like those on these peasants' hats, became a symbol of commitment to the Revolution.

Each sex is called to the kind of occupation which is fitting for it; its action is circumscribed within this circle which it cannot break through because nature, which has imposed these limits on mankind, commands imperiously and receives no law. . . . Women are disposed by their constitution to an overexcitation which would be deadly in public affairs. . . . [Women] are ill suited for elevated thoughts and serious meditation.[20]

The next day, Amar's eloquent speech against political women prompted the Convention to pass a decree banning all women's clubs. According to the Convention, women were not made for militant political action, and their participation in the Revolution should be limited to providing support as determined by male revolutionary leaders. The market women of Paris had scored a victory, and the Society of Revolutionary Republican Women ceased to exist.

The Hunger of 1794

Food shortages grew severe in early 1794. Many families had to live on bread alone. Women desperate to secure a bit of bread formed lines at bakeries in the middle of the night. The crowds in front of these shops often grew unruly. One police spy gave the following report of a breadline on the Rue Montorgueil that formed in the evening of February 26:

These were not cries but howls, or more accurately, an atrocious roar of rage. Paris in counterrevolution presented nothing more horrible. The women fought among themselves for the right to reach the place of distribution. Several women before me had been struck by kicks and punches, thrown out of lines, and

Women of the French Revolution

dragged in the gutter. Others cried loudly for revolt, which perhaps would have occurred if the volunteers and the police on horseback had not arrived to repress all these seditious movements.[21]

For most of the city's working women, life at this time came down to necessities of bare survival. Factories closed, causing widespread unemployment. Raw materials—such as thread for seamstresses and soap for

Careless Words

In the streets of revolutionary Paris, ordinary people—who normally had very little to do with politics—learned to choose their words carefully. During a frustrating wait in line for food in September 1794, Anne Felicite Guinee, a twenty-four-year-old wigmaker's wife, found herself under arrest for making the wrong remarks to a government official. Quoted on the Web site *Liberty, Equality, Fraternity*, Guinee herself describes the scene in her petition for freedom.

I was compelled to go wait in line to get something to eat. For three days I had been going to the same market without being able to get anything, despite the fact that I had waited from 7 or 8 A.M. until 5 or 6 P.M. After the distribution of butter on the twenty-second, some citizens said to me, "Are you still here?" I replied, "For three days I have been coming without getting the least thing." A citizen came over to me and said that I was in very delicate condition. To that I answered, "You can't be

delicate and be on your legs for so long. I wouldn't have come if there were any other food." He replied that I needed to drink milk. I answered that I had men in my house who worked and that I couldn't nourish them with milk, that I was convinced that if he, the speaker, were sensitive to the difficulty of obtaining food, he would not vex me so, and that he was an imbecile and wanted to play despot, and no one had that right. Here, on the spot, I was arrested and brought to the guard house. I wanted to explain myself. I was silenced and dragged off to prison. . . .

I was taken to the Revolutionary Committee of my Section, which without waiting to hear me, had me taken to the Mairie, where I stayed for nine days without a bed or a chair with vermin and with women addicted to all sorts of crimes who wanted everything from me. And when I complained, they put a knife to my throat.

A group of women assembles outside a bakery during the 1794 food shortages. A lack of basic necessities was a fact of daily life for many during the Revolution.

laundrywomen—grew extremely scarce. The value of the assignat, the revolutionary–era currency, fell to a small fraction of its face value. Price controls were lifted, putting many food staples out of reach for artisans and factory workers. And food shortages continued, worsened by freezing winter weather that turned the Seine River to a sheet of ice, which prevented supply barges from reaching the capital.

Women who still supported the radical Jacobins fought tooth and nail with counterrevolutionaries and the Girondins, many of whom had returned to the capital. They disrupted meetings of the Convention, which was now attempting to repress the Jacobins. In May 1795, the Parisian militants carried out a general insurrection against the Convention. Women led mobs that churned through the city, dragooning passersby into their companies and attacking suspected bourgeois opponents. In the Convention hall, women shouted down the speakers, rushed the doors, and fought in the hallways with policemen. They confronted the deputy Jean Feraud, their outspoken opponent, and dragged him from his chair; then they struck him with their wooden clogs, shot him, and cut off his head. A newspaper account described the trouble in the Convention galleries: "The cries 'for bread for bread' began again. Attempts to calm the women were in vain; some laughed at the state in which they saw the Convention; while others waved their fists at the president and the other representatives of the people. Their example spread; the second gallery on the other side also filled with women who uttered the same cry."[22]

Repression of the female militants followed. Women were banned from the Convention and from any and all political assemblies. About 150 were arrested and prosecuted for taking part in the insurgency. The wives of the radical "Montagnard" deputies, who had incited attacks on the Girondins and other moderates, were simply deported from the city. The Convention unanimously prohibited women from gathering in public in groups larger than five individuals, declaring:

Whether misguided or incited by enemies of liberty, women abuse the regards we have for the weakness of their sex, run through the streets, assemble, form up in ranks, and create disorder in all the operations of the police and military. [Therefore] we decree that all women withdraw, until otherwise ordered, to their respective homes. Those women who, one hour after the posting of the present decree, are found in the streets, gathered in groups of more than five, will be dispersed by armed force and then arrested.[23]

The repression of 1795 marked the end of the militants' revolution. Paris and the rest of France were reeling from six years of violence, fear, and hunger. The zeal of the female militants of Paris for liberty and republican government settled, for most of them, into a daily effort to survive, find employment, and regain stability. Nevertheless, their ardor had helped bring about an important political transformation and would be recalled in the mythical figure of Marianne, a powerful symbol of female revolutionary zeal that emerged during the Revolution and has survived as a national symbol of France.

Chapter 3:
Women of the Societies

Political activity of any kind was a novelty for the women of revolutionary France. In the late eighteenth century, the majority of French men and women of all classes still believed that a woman's place was in the home. This view did not discourage a few female pioneers from forming their own political clubs, or founding women's sections of the men-only clubs. The revolution that began in 1789 allowed the women of these clubs to express their grievances and demands to the men of the legislatures. But for many nonmembers, the clubs grew too strong. This belief led to a decisive confrontation among women in the fall of 1793.

Forming clubs and societies in and of itself was not a novelty in eighteenth-century France. Workers of both sexes organized themselves in labor cooperatives and guilds. Men gathered in private social clubs, while women attended meetings of charitable clubs. Although many clubs banned political talk, the government of Louis XVI saw them as a threat as tensions rose in the 1780s, and

in 1787 social clubs were temporarily outlawed. After the calling of the Estates General in May 1789, France experienced a wave of enthusiasm for political debate. Hundreds of political clubs formed in cities large and small all over the kingdom. Members of the National Assembly established one of these clubs in Paris, where they met three times a week at a Jacobin monastery on the Rue St. Honore in the center of the city. For two years after the imprisonment of King Louis XVI, the leaders of this group, known as Jacobins, would control the French Revolution.

The Jacobin club was for men only, an accepted practice supported by the writings of philosopher Jean-Jacques Rousseau, the most popular writer of the day. Rousseau argued for the equality of all citizens and the idea that kings ruled as representatives of the will of the people. But Rousseau also believed that women could best find happiness in domestic life, in providing for their families and by staying out of the rough-and-tumble world of business and politics.

Rousseau's philosophy did not discourage a few women from plunging into the revolutionary debate. Although the Jacobins banned women from becoming members, they sold tickets to women so they could observe the meetings from the galleries. And on rare occasions, they allowed spirited revolutionary women, such as Theroigne de Mericourt, to deliver a speech.

In 1790 Le Confederation des Amis de la Verite, or Confederation of the Friends of Truth, formed a women's section led by Etta Palm d'Aelders. The members met every Monday and Friday in underground chambers of the Palais Royale in Paris. The confederation sought complete equality for women in matters of divorce, inheritance, and suffrage (the right to vote). It had more than three thousand members just a few weeks after it formed. But it also set its dues at eight livres a month—an expense meant to attract women of the upper classes.

A contemporary painting depicts a meeting of a patriotic women's club. Similar clubs were formed through France during the late 1780s.

One of the most popular speakers at meetings of the Friends of Truth was the Marquis de Condorcet. In July 1790, the marquis published a powerful appeal for women's equal rights, mentioning an important principle that inspired the American Revolution. In her article "Feminism in the French Revolution," author Jean Abray describes Condorcet's positions:

> He reasoned that women, since they were not allowed to vote, were being taxed without representation and would be justified in refusing to pay their taxes. Morever, said Condorcet, domestic authority should be shared and all positions and professions opened to both sexes. He observed that sexual inequality was a new state and not the traditional lot of women. A year later Condorcet insisted that women who met the property qualifications he proposed for the suffrage should vote. He also predicted that his ideas would get little support from women, as they were all too enamored of Jean-Jacques Rousseau to listen to him.[24]

The Cercle Social

The words of the marquis gained a widespread appreciation and helped to inspire the forming of a club known as the Cercle Social, which admitted women as dues-paying members. The Cercle Social was known for its political debates and philosophical discussions. But it took a more active role through its newspaper, the *Bouche de Fer*, or *Mouth of Iron*. The name referred to a small iron box installed in the newspaper's offices, in which anyone might deposit a complaint or condemn an enemy of the Revolution, anonymously, assured that soon afterward the grievance would appear in the newspaper's columns.

A separate women's section of the Cercle Social was established in March 1791 to argue for a reform of the laws of divorce and property ownership. In the meantime, a few more inclusive political clubs, including the Cordeliers of Paris, were admitting women to their ranks. Claude Dansard, a schoolteacher, founded the Fraternal Society of Patriots of Both Sexes, which included the chocolate maker Pauline Leon, the historian Louise de Keralio, Theroigne de Mericourt, and Etta Palm d'Aelders. According to Simon Schama, these inclusive societies provided women with an effective voice in the ongoing political debate:

> It was from these clubs that proposals emanated to form companies of armed women—for example, to guard the royal family in the Tuileries in 1791 and as a frontier regiment in

A Proposal for Action

❧

Inspired by the forming of the first women's political societies in the spring of 1791, Etta Palm d'Aelders wrote a pamphlet calling for an entire network of such clubs, which would gather in every section (neighborhood) in Paris. In this long pamphlet, quoted in *Women in Revolutionary Paris 1789–1795*, she spelled out her program for action for the revolutionary women of France.

Would it not be useful to form, in each Section of the capital, a patriotic society of citoyennes, female friends of the truth? . . . Each circle of citoyennes would meet in each Section as frequently as they believed useful for the public good and following their own particular rules; each circle would have its own directorate, which would meet once a week. . . .

These societies of citoyennes could be charged, in addition, with supervising public education. Wouldn't it be natural that charity schools, given over for the most part to ignorant people brought up with all kinds of prejudices, be under the immediate supervision of enlightened and virtuous citoyennes? Zealous women patriots would take care to teach children the rights of men, respect and obedience for the law. . . .

These women's clubs could be charged in addition with investigating the conduct and the need of unfortunate people requesting aid from the Section. . . . Commissioners would be charged with going into humble dwellings to inform themselves concerning morals, conduct, or misfortune of the indigent and with bringing consolation along with aid to their unfortunate brothers. In this way the distance between the rich and the poor would be narrowed infinitely. In this way charity would be excited in the one, courage and patience in the other. The morals of both would be purified and egoism destroyed, and the wealthy man, object of jealousy and envy, would become an object of love and veneration to his brother in indigence.

1792—as well as reiterations of the demands first articulated by Olympe de Gouges and Etta Palm D'Aelders for female suffrage. They took exception to the typical Jacobin relegation of women to the hearth and home and comments like that of the brewer Santerre that "the men of this district

Women of the Societies

prefer on coming home from work to find their household in order rather than to see their wives returning from an assembly where they do not always acquire a spirit of gentleness."[25]

As defense of the Revolution became a priority for radical revolutionaries, women called for legal standing equal to that of men. They were to be sorely disappointed by the constitution passed in September 1791, in which the people of France were divided into "active" and "passive" citizens—the latter group including all women, regardless of their social rank or wealth.

On March 9, 1792, Pauline Leon led a group of women to the Legislative Assembly to present a petition demanding permission to bear arms and to organize a female national guard. In her address, Leon stated:

> We want only to defend ourselves as you do. . . . You cannot refuse, and society cannot deny, the right nature gives us, unless you pretend that the Declaration of Rights does not apply to women and that they should let their throats be cut, without the right to defend themselves. For can you believe the tyrants would spare us? No! No!—they remember October fifth and sixth [1789].[26]

The Assembly was thrown into confusion. After a short debate, the members simply declared that the petition should be printed, and then proceeded to the next order of business. In June 1792, another petition was presented by women to the Assembly, this one demanding the punishment of all counterrevolutionary conspirators. Like all other petitions presented by the women of Paris, this demand fell on deaf ears; the men of the Assembly saw Leon and other female petitioners as an amusing spectacle and little else. They were wrong to ignore her, however. After the execution of the king in 1793, Leon and the actress Claire Lacombe organized another club that would become the most influential women's organization of the entire Revolution.

The Society of Revolutionary Republican Women

Born in 1768, Pauline Leon was a chocolate maker who lived with her parents on the Rue de Grenelle, on the Left (southern) Bank of the Seine River in Paris. She had taken part in the storming of the Bastille in July 1789, inciting crowds and collecting paving stones and other missiles to use against the prison walls and gate. In June 1791, she had nearly been murdered by a company of royal guards when she spoke out against the king's attempt to flee the country. She had also come under fire on July 17, 1791, on the Champ de Mars, after signing the petition for the abolition of the monarchy. She had also signed petitions demanding women's right to bear arms as well as a petition for the execution of the king.

Claire Lacombe was a successful actress from the southern port town of Marseille. She abandoned her career and arrived in Paris in March 1792, ready to dedicate herself to the Revolution. She helped lead the assault on the Tuileries palace on August 10, 1792, and her bravery on that date established her reputation throughout the city.

In February 1793, Leon and Lacombe formed the Societe des Citoyennes Republicaines Revolutionnaires, or Society of Revolutionary Republican Women. The society declared itself to the authorities on May 10, 1793, and announced that its meetings would take place at the library of the Jacobin convent on the Rue Saint Honore. On May 12, members met to proclaim their intention to arrest and disarm enemies of the Revolution. They insisted on the right of women to bear arms, sought to reform the penal system, favored price controls on staples such as bread and sugar, and set up a program to educate prostitutes in order to bring them into the social mainstream.

Not content to simply debate and present petitions to the authorities, the members of the society advanced their political agenda in the streets of Paris. Historian Joan Landes explains:

> All members of the Society affected a kind of uniform, appearing in public in the red bonnet, with tricolor ribbon, and trousers. They carried arms, usually a pistol and dagger. In this faction, the Revolutionary Republicans policed the streets and markets and attended the galleries in the fashion of a revolutionary army, as would a general and her troops.[27]

The women of the society proudly wore the red liberty cap and the revolutionary cockade. Bearing knives and pistols in defiance of the laws, they seized aristocrats and suspected food hoarders, bringing them before the revolutionary courts to face justice.

In the spring of 1793, the conflict between the Girondins (led by Condorcet and Jacques Pierre Brissot) and the Montagnards (headed by Robespierre) in the Convention intensified, and women of the society played a prominent role. They gathered before the legislature and harangued the crowds, inciting them against the moderate Girondin faction. They demanded the removal and arrest of the Girondin

Pauline Leon and other members of the Society of Revolutionary Republican Women urge the Convention to purge members of the Girondin faction.

deputies. They entered the galleries and hooted at and heckled Girondin speakers, lustily cheering on the Montagnards. Society women patrolled the halls of the legislature, blocking the galleries that the Girondin faction had reserved for their friends and allies.

The fight against the Girondins in Paris grew violent in May. The Girondin deputies were ousted from the Convention in early June, rounded up, and led to the guillotine. Late that summer the Society of Revolutionary Republican Women began calling for a campaign of terror against all counterrevolutionaries and food hoarders. When price controls were imposed by the legislature, they demanded strict surveillance of the marketplaces to enforce the controls. They broke into the debates of the Cordeliers club as well as the Jacobins. They directly confronted and intimidated the Jacobin leaders who they felt did not show the proper revolutionary zeal.

The Society Declares Itself

On July 9, the Society of Revolutionary Republican Women formally adopted a set of written regulations. In the preamble to this document, the members set down a vision of the future, in which evil intentions and motivations would be banished forever:

> Convinced that there is no liberty without customs and principles, and that one must recognize one's social duties in order to fulfill one's domestic duties adequately, the Revolutionary Republican *citoyennes* have formed a Society to instruct themselves, to learn well the Constitution and laws of the Republic, to attend to public affairs, to succor suffering humanity, and to defend all human beings who become victims of any arbitrary acts whatsoever. They

A Girondin Witness

As one of its first actions, the Society of Revolutionary Republican Women supported the purge of the Girondin deputies from the National Convention. In a pamphlet written in June 1793, one of these deputies, A.J. Gorsas, voiced his dismay at the actions of these feminine upstarts, as quoted in *Women in Revolutionary Paris 1789–1795*.

A muffled fermentation, moreover, prevails in Paris. Some women meet, undoubtedly excited by the furies; they are armed with pistols and daggers; they make declarations and rush to all the public places in the city, bearing before them the standard of license. In vain is this crime denounced to the Commune; in vain does one wish to escape dangerous consequences. . . . These drunken bacchanalians have been received in the midst of the General Council; there they have been greeted, feted, and given the fraternal accolade. And what do they want, what do they demand? They want to "put an end to it," they want to "purge the Convention, to make heads roll, and to get themselves drunk with blood."

want to banish all selfishness, jealousies, rivalry, and envy and to make good their name.[28]

The club had about two hundred members; prospective members had to be at least eighteen years old, sponsored by a member of the society, and supported by two others. The society was led by a president, vice president, and four secretaries. By Article V of the regulations, to keep order in the often unruly meetings, "The President will wear the bonnet of liberty, and the two monitors will wear a ribbon of the nation on their left arm. When the President is unable to establish order with the bell, she will take off her bonnet; then all the *citoyennes* will rise and remain standing until she puts her bonnet on again."[29]

The society affiliated itself with the Jacobin cause and demanded price controls and a tax on the rich. But its primary mission was to combat enemies of the Revolution. As the National Guard and army would fight external enemies, the members of the club would fight within the nation's borders to root out and exterminate all counterrevolutionaries. They planned to form companies of fighting women, send them to the streets of the cities and to the front lines, and lay the enemies of the Revolution at their feet.

Through the summer of 1793, the society attracted scant attention from the men who were then in control of the Revolution and fighting for power and influence. Though the Assembly ignored its proposals, the society's meetings often attracted men who came to jeer and ridicule them. In his memoirs, author Pierre Roussel described one meeting that he attended as a visitor. The meeting was held in a long, vaulted room that was once an ossuary (a storage chamber for human skeletons). With sixty-seven members of the society in attendance, visitors stood at one end of the room and watched from behind a bar.

Roussel watched as the last minutes were read aloud, and a member by the name of Monic spoke of the deeds of famous women warriors of the past: the biblical Deborah, Joan of Arc, and the women who took part in the march to Versailles in 1789. The society proposed to raise an army of warriors, to admit women into all departments of the republican administration, and to present a petition to the legislature calling for the compulsory wearing of the revolutionary cockade. Finally, Olympe de Gouges, author of the Declaration of the Rights of Woman, rose to speak. She described women's ability to inspire men to courageous and heroic deeds and added:

A family registers with a revolutionary committee in this contemporary sketch. The primary purpose of such committees was to combat enemies of the Revolution.

Here is what I have thought up: If there are no longer any processions, there will have to be public festivals; confide the direction and regulation of them to us. . . . Let us request the direction of festivals and marriages, and that we be the only ones charged with the education of youth. This is all the more easily done, as the priests, whose privilege this used to be (for reasons I cannot fathom), are no longer here. It is up to us to replace them, and to found the religion of the true sans-culottes.[30]

Roussel and his companion, the English Lord Bedford, found the speeches of the women both amusing and alarming:

The Englishman said to me:—Confess that these extravagances are very amusing.—I confess, but when I think about it, the delirium of these women frightens me. If their brains are overheated, you know the obstinacy of their sex; they are capable of committing certain excesses.

—Your nation possesses the remedy: the weapon of ridicule and banter, which it knows so well how to wield, will destroy these comical pretensions. Among the follies we have just heard, one can find nothing based in reason.[31]

Men on the Counterattack

Participating in political debate was something new for the women of eighteenth-century France. By the 1770s, women who were beginning to speak out, in salons and in public, were drawing angry attention from male writers such as the popular novelist Restif de la Bretonne. In an effort to put things right, Bretonne wrote a book of essays, *Gynographes*, in 1776 and subtitled it *Project for Regulations to All Europe, to Put Women Back in Their Place and by Such Means Work Efficiently Toward the Reform of Morals.*

Claire Lacombe's gifts as a speaker and her dedication to the Revolution and the Jacobin cause raised her to the position of president. But after reading the club's petition of August 26 to the Convention, she came under attack by the Jacobins, who saw her eloquence as a serious threat. Jacobin leaders ordered her arrest but then released her after police searched her home and found no evidence that she was a counterrevolutionary.

The Society Is Banned

The revolutionary fervor was bringing a reaction in the fall of 1793, when the society petitioned the legislature to force the wearing of the revolutionary cockade. The atmosphere in Paris and in the Convention was growing increasingly tense, with many deputies fearing execution merely for a lack of enthusiasm. The measure was passed. But when the society then proposed a new law for the reform and education of prostitutes, the Convention, then in the hands of the Jacobins, refused to cooperate.

In the meantime, the edict on the wearing of the cockade was provoking brawls in the marketplaces of Paris. Provocateurs appeared on the streets to take advantage of the situation and sow dissension. These men, who dressed as common laborers, encouraged the women to rebel against the revolutionary leaders by insisting on women's rights, according to one police report:

These enemies of public tranquillity flatter the pride of women, seeking to persuade them that they have as many rights as men in the government of their country; that the right to vote in elections is a natural right they should demand; that in a state where law consecrates equality, women may claim all civilian and military employment; that things would doubtless go much better if affairs were conducted by good republican women....That is a summary of a very long and most carefully worked out discourse which yesterday was spouted by a young dandy, disguised in the costume of a sans-culotte, in the presence of some women. . . . But he lost the whole fruit of his anarchic eloquence; they listened to him nearly as one would listen to a charlatan who dispensed his balm, and they withdrew before anyone appeared to try to put his prescription to use.[32]

When the society ended its support for the Jacobin faction, the stage was set for a showdown. The market women of Paris, angered by the police surveillance of their trade, confronted the cockade wearers, assaulting the women and throwing their bonnets, liberty caps, and cockades into the mud. In October a mob of market women stormed a meeting of the society, brawling with its members and beating several of them senseless. They then petitioned the Convention to dissolve the society and ban all women's political clubs.

This particular women's petition drew interest and eventual approval by the Convention, and the Society of Revolutionary Republican Women was officially outlawed. From the rostrum of the Convention, several representatives scolded women for their meddling in men's affairs, and women found themselves restricted to the galleries of the legislature, reduced to powerless observers.

With the ban on women's clubs, direct political activity by women in France was extinguished. The Terror then beginning in Paris was making any kind of public speaking or political action extremely unwise and often fatal, as small factions of the Jacobins fought each other with arrest warrants and the guillotine. After the ban of October 30, Pauline Leon returned to her chocolate business and withdrew from public life. Soon afterward, she was arrested with her husband, writer Theophile Leclerc, in the town of Lafere, but was later released, after which she disappeared from history. After being denounced by several other members of the society, Claire Lacombe was arrested again and held in prison for fifteen months. Three months after her release, she left Paris for Nantes, where she returned to her livelihood as a dramatic actress.

But Lacombe, Leon, and other outspoken women had left their mark on the Revolution. They had demonstrated that women could organize themselves and argue for their rights and ideals, even in the midst of a violent social upheaval. They had also shown that they would fight. Although not all women favored this surprising new stance among the "passive" gender, most felt more liberty to express their views to neighbors and to family. Supporting this new role were several eloquent women who were making themselves heard via the Revolution's favored communications medium—the written word.

Chapter 4:
Women Writers

In prerevolutionary France, very few women published books, pamphlets, or plays. Literacy among women lagged far behind that of men; most women who could write could only sign their name. French society looked on women as eloquent speakers but not as capable writers—until the Revolution. This event freed women from the legal restrictions on their right to publish their works. As a result, many articulate women expressed strong opinions and drew the public spotlight through the written word. But public attention also brought very real dangers, and for some revolutionary women the power of the written word proved fatal.

Before the Revolution, even a talented woman who had something to express in words faced obstacles. Written works of any kind were not considered the private property of authors who created them. Instead, literary works were believed to be inspired by God and could be published only through a *privilege d'auteur* granted by a ministry of the king, God's representative on earth. The royal administration held the right to censor any works it deemed sacrilegious or otherwise unfit for the public. The privilege, held jointly by the author and publisher, granted the author exclusive rights to publish and profit from a book, but also ended with the death of the author.

Under the Old Regime, married women did not have the right to sign contracts on their own. Their husbands held legal control over their works, and without a husband's consent, a woman could not publish anything. Only men wrote books, according to the traditions of the publishing guilds (private trade associations), and for this reason most women who did manage to publish did so anonymously or under a male pen name. In any case, the vast majority of men and women of France did not find writing a suitable occupation for women. To express ideas and creativity in written form did not fit with the traditional notions of women: the gentle and modest half of humanity, properly content to simply support their husbands and family. In the words of the most famous writer of the Revolution, Germaine de Staël:

Men and women of the aristocracy participate in a literary circle. During the Revolution, women were encouraged to write and publish their works.

Women of the French Revolution

The spirit of chivalry, still lingering on in France, was opposed in some respects to the overeager cultivation of letters even by men; it must have aroused all the more dislike for women concentrating on literary studies and turning their thoughts away from their primary concern, the sentiments of the heart . . . Women were certainly allowed to sacrifice household occupations to a love of society and its pleasures; serious study, however, was condemned as pedantic.[33]

For many women, the only outlet for their interest in writing and the expression of ideas was the private salon. At these upper-class gatherings, women served as arbiters of fashion and good taste. Writers came to promote their books and debate the ideas those books contained. The female hosts encouraged those writers they favored and introduced them to influential guests, who could spread enthusiasm for new books and plays to the general public. Writers who found themselves disinvited from a weekly salon found their careers languishing and their books going unsold.

The Revolution Frees French Writers

During the Revolution, the influence of the salon and of aristocratic taste began to wane. Newspapers and pamphlets bringing news of the Revolution reached a wider audience, who followed closely the debates of competing leaders and factions. Several women emerged as leading voices of the revolutionary movement, and newspapers were published specifically for women, including *L'Etoile du Matin*, a journal edited by Madame de Verte Allure, a former nun, and *La Gazette des Halles*, a journal for the women of the marketplaces. Female authors contributed articles to these papers, female printers created them, and women of means supported them. Louise de Keralio, a noted historian, wrote articles and edited *Le Mercure Nationale*, one of the most popular newspapers of the time.

At the same time, the Revolution radically changed the legal rights of authors, both male and female. Royal censorship ended with the Declaration of the Rights of Man and of the Citizen, passed by the National Assembly on August 26, 1789. This proclamation declared freedom of expression of the spoken and written word. In 1791 the legislature lifted restrictions on membership in the guilds, ending centuries of tradition. This action opened trades such as book publishing to women. A law of June 1793 allowed women to sign contracts and recognized their property rights, even within marriage. In July the Declaration of the Rights of Genius recognized male and female authors as the sole legal owners of their works. According to the new law, property rights in written works would last for the lifetime of the author plus ten years.

Still, many men of the time were outraged by the pretensions of women who presumed to write books as if they had the education and careful, level-headed moral judgment of men. In his book *Tableau de Paris*, Louis-Sebastien Mercier wrote:

> What claim to fame has the woman who suddenly decides to make her entrance into the sanctuary of the muses and philosophy? She has ogled, bantered, simpered, made silk knots and little nothings. She has wasted her mind in a sea of futility; she has only noticed glitter and has always been content with superficiality; she has blinded herself; yet she believes that she can judge a book as she can a pompom. Her mind's laziness prevents her from analyzing; her short supply of mental energy does not permit her to understand the important elements of a work; her flightiness alights on some details and cannot take in the whole idea; she articulates the same way as she feels, in a vague, uncertain and ambiguous manner.[34]

With such a prevailing attitude, the vast majority of Frenchwomen did not even consider writing as a career. Although many literate women read novels, kept diaries, and wrote letters, only women of the aristocracy, for the most part, took an interest in literature. One such woman, Madame Necker, the wife of Jacques Necker, hosted one of the most prestigious salons in Paris. She also had an ambition to write, but her husband disapproved and prevented her from publishing her works. Their daughter, however, would not be dissuaded. A novelist and dramatist as well as a brilliant critic and essayist, Anne-Louis-Germaine de Staël would emerge as the leading chronicler, male or female, of the revolutionary years.

Germaine de Staël

After the fall of the Bastille, popular discontent with the dismissal of Jacques Necker as minister of finances persuaded Louis XVI to change his mind and recall Necker to Paris. On July 30, 1789, Germaine de Staël witnessed her father's hero's welcome at the Hotel de Ville. When Necker and his family were exiled once again, his daughter returned on her own to Paris from Switzerland and set up her own salon in the capital. In the winter of 1791–1792, Germaine de Staël became a true power broker, promoting men

whose views she favored at her popular salon. Nevertheless, according to Winifred Stephens,

> Mme de Stael, one of the most brilliant talkers that ever lived . . . was not an ideal salonniere. She was too restless, too impulsive, too loquacious. The business of a salon lady is not so much to talk herself as to make her guests talk, to draw them out and set them at their ease. . . . Neither did she possess that other quality, so indispensable in every good hostess—the quality of tact.[35]

Madame de Staël had one other flaw: Like every other revolutionary leader, she could not remain neutral as revolutionary factions fought for power. When the radical Jacobin party rose in power, her support of a constitutional monarchy went out of fashion and by the fall of 1792 had become extremely dangerous. After the September massacres in 1792, when the aristocracy experienced a mortal fear of imprisonment and execution, Staël tried to flee Paris. Her carriage was stopped by an angry mob and she was forced to return to the capital. Eventually, she did escape, only to return in the fall of 1796.

As a powerful writer and influential *salonniere*, Staël was much feared by the Directory, the government set up in the wake of the Revolution. Not wanting any trouble or criticism from this influential woman, the Directory deported her again as an illegal foreigner. Although she had been born in France, by the laws of her native country, her nationality was determined first by that of her father—who was Swiss—and second by her husband, a Swedish diplomat whom she had married while still a legal minor.

Staël's book of essays, *Considerations sur les principaux evenements de la Revolution Francaise,* was published in 1818. In *Considerations*, she describes how, during the French Revolution, the desire for reform unleashed the terrible jealousy felt by members of one class for the one standing above it:

A sort of fury took hold of the poor in the presence of the rich; as the jealousy inspired by property was reinforced by aristocratic distinctions, the people grew proud of their own

numbers. . . . Mutual antipathy was stronger in France than elsewhere because there was almost no connection among the different classes of society. If one knows someone personally, even the most criminal of men, one cannot hate him in quite the same way as if one were imagining him. Pride had set up barriers everywhere, and limits nowhere. . . . The elegance of the French nobility increased the envy it inspired. Its manners were as hard to imitate as its prerogatives were to gain. And the same scene was repeated on every step of the scale. The irritability of an ultrasensitive nation made everyone jealous of his neighbor, of his superior, of his master. Not content with domination, all those individuals humiliated each other.[36]

Under the reign of Napoléon Bonaparte, who seized power in a coup d'état in 1799, Germaine de Staël again found herself on the wrong side of authority. Napoléon exiled her again, freeing her to turn her sharp pen and wit against the self-proclaimed emperor of the French. Although she hated the violence and political fanaticism of the Revolution, she also felt contempt for the reaction of the Napoleonic years, when new laws again placed numerous restrictions

A Revolutionary Model Marriage Contract

Revolutionary women had novel ideas not only for women's rights to vote and to claim property but also on the institution of marriage. In the Declaration of the Rights of Woman and the Female Citizen, quoted on the Web site *Modern History Sourcebook*, Olympe de Gouges sets out her future ideal of marriage, property rights, and inheritance.

We, _____ and _____, moved by our own will, unite ourselves for the duration of our lives, and for the duration of our mutual inclinations, under the following conditions: We intend and wish to make our wealth communal, meanwhile reserving to ourselves the right to divide it in favor of our children and of those toward whom we might have a particular inclination, mutually recognizing that our property belongs directly to our children, from whatever bed they come, and that all of them without distinction have the right to bear the name of the fathers and mothers who have acknowledged them, and we are charged to subscribe to the law which punishes the renunciation of one's own blood. We likewise obligate ourselves, in case of separation, to divide our wealth and to set aside in advance the portion the law indicates for our children, and in the event of a perfect union, the one who dies will divest himself of half his property in his children's favor, and if one dies childless, the survivor will inherit by right, unless the dying person has disposed of half the common property in favor of one whom he judged deserving.

Olympe de Gouges championed the rights of women during the Revolution.

on women and made book publishing all but illegal for female authors.

Louise de Keralio

While Germaine de Staël came from an influential family, Louise de Keralio had not only the advantage of nobility but also the luck to have two writers for parents. Her father wrote military histories, and her mother wrote novels (anonymously). This combination of history and imagination inspired Keralio herself to fashion a new writing style that made her one of the most respected authors of eighteenth-century France.

The Robespierre Sister

Historians found in Charlotte Robespierre, the sister of Maximilien Robespierre, one of the most interesting chroniclers of the Revolution. Actually a quiet and modest woman, Charlotte had no writing ambition and was known to be a contented helpmate to her brothers Maximilien and Augustin. She lived with Maximilien in Arras when he was an unknown lawyer, and she moved with him to Paris when he was attending the Estates General. During the Terror, Charlotte Robespierre steadfastly stood by her brother, even as he came under attack in the summer of 1794. Quoted by Marilyn Yalom in *Blood Sisters*, in her memoirs Charlotte describes a despairing search for her brother after the July coup that brought him down:

The next day, the tenth of Thermidor, I rush into the streets, my head full of anxiety. I look for my brothers. I learn that they have been taken to the Conciergerie. I run there, ask to see them, plead with folded hands, get down on my knees in front of the soldiers. They push me away, laugh at my tears, insult me, strike me. Several people, moved by pity, drag me away. My reason became clouded. I no longer knew what was happening, what would become of me. Or rather, I found out several days later; when I came to myself, I was in prison.

Despite Charlotte's entreaties, Maximilien and Augustin Robespierre went to the scaffold. After Maximilien's execution, Charlotte Robespierre defiantly defended her brother's name. But Maximilien had left nothing behind for the sister who survived him. By a strange irony of history, she was kept alive by a pension granted by the next two monarchs of France: Napoléon Bonaparte and King Louis XVIII.

In 1782, at the age of twenty-four, Louise de Keralio published an anonymous novel, written in the form of a memoir, titled *Adelaide ou les memoirs de la marquise de*—- (*Adelaide or Memoirs of the Marquise de*—-). The next year, when she reached her legal age of majority as an unmarried woman, she began receiving the *privilege d'auteur*, which allowed her to publish her works.

In 1787 she published a five-volume biography of England's Queen Elizabeth, thus trespassing into the men's domain of history. In this work, she argued that Elizabeth, by placing the state firmly ahead of the church, had been the true founder of the modern constitutional monarchy. Her book reached a wide audience and prompted the literary academy of the town of Arras to admit her as a member. On her admission, the president of the academy, Maximilien Robespierre, expressed his support for women writers—a stand that would bring Keralio's later support for Robespierre while he served as a deputy in the national legislature.

In August 1789, Keralio founded the *Journal de l'Etat et du Citoyen* (*Journal of the State and of the Citizen*). She followed events as a journalist, but daring to express political opinions drew criticism, according to Carla Hesse:

By the end of October 1789 she found herself publicly characterized by radical journalists as a "*phenomene politique*" and an "*amazone.*" Moreover, by 1789 Keralio was thirty-one years old and still single. She was thus becoming increasingly vulnerable to the threat of social marginalization as a "*vieille fille*" (old maid). Indeed, hostile pamphleteers were already beginning to attach the stereotypical attributes of the "*vieille fille*"—"*laide*" (ugly), "*susceptible aux fureurs uterines*" (prone to uterine hysteria)—to her name.[37]

In December 1789, Keralio folded the *Journal de l'Etat* and founded the *Mercure Nationale.* In 1790 she married a Jacobin, Francois Robert. As Madame Robert, she began to withdraw from the public scene as a reaction set in against the feminine revolutionary vanguard. In the streets and assemblies, in the view of many, women were stirring up trouble, and Keralio came to agree with this view.

This view did not stop Keralio from writing, however, and in 1791 she anonymously published *Les Crimes des Reines de France* (*The Crimes of the Queens of France*). Using the example of history's bad queens, she made the point that queens are by and large immoral and dangerous because their power lies outside of the law and they exercise this power by influencing their husbands, the kings, to unwise actions. As for Marie-Antoinette, Keralio depicted her as a wastrel and as a meddler in public affairs, working and scheming behind the scenes to manipulate the king and help the ministers she favored.

With this book Keralio withdrew from writing altogether. Despite her known sympathies with the political conservatives, she survived the Revolution. Other women writers, including the *salonniere* and memoirist known as Madame Roland, were not so lucky.

The Fatal Opinions of Madame Roland

Madame Roland arrived in Paris with her husband, a deputy to the Assembly from Lyon, in February 1791. She soon became one of the city's favorite *salonnieres.* Madame Roland hosted her husband's Girondin colleagues several times a week. While the men would avidly discuss politics and the future of the nation, she sat silently, attending to her letters or her knitting and listening to the arguments. Madame Roland believed women had no proper role in public life and saw the wife's role as being a domestic helpmate and supporter of her husband and his career. Although she had a passion for writing, she never had her own words published, fearing the ridicule and criticism that might greet her pretensions as an author.

In March 1792, after joining the Jacobin society, Monsieur Roland was appointed by Louis XVI as minister of the interior. At this time, the king was seeking to show magnanimity and compromise by appointing Jacobins to his cabinet. But in June Roland wrote a public letter to the king opposing his failure to approve two decrees passed by the Assembly and was promptly dismissed (only to be restored to the post after the overthrow of the king in August). The letter to the king was in fact written by Madame Roland.

Her sympathies with the Girondin faction were well known, and Madame Roland did not stop her criticisms of the radical Jacobins. A few days after the execution of the king, on January 21, 1793, her husband, accused of loyalty to the monarchy, resigned his post. On May 31, while Girondin deputies were being purged from the Convention, a warrant for his arrest was issued. Although Roland fled Paris, his wife remained behind, convinced she could win an acquittal by speaking out in support of him. On June 1, she was arrested and thrown into the Abbaye prison.

The police brought no charges against Madame Roland until July 1793. In that month, after Charlotte Corday's assassination of Jean-Paul Marat, it was discovered that Corday had visited a Girondist deputy named Duperret.

Madame Roland hosts a group of Girondins in her Paris salon. As a vociferous supporter of the Girondin faction, Roland was arrested and executed by the radical Jacobins.

When the police searched Duperret's house, letters from Madame Roland were found. This was enough evidence to charge her with conspiracy against the government.

While in prison, Madame Roland began writing letters, as well as note-books, in which she poured out a bitter attack on her political enemies. She smuggled these writings out to a friend, who, fearing for his life if the notebooks should be discovered, burned most of them. She then began working on a personal memoir, an autobiography that

During her imprisonment, Madame Roland wrote a memoir that attacked Jacobin leaders and blamed them for the Revolution.

began with her childhood. She bitterly attacked radical leaders, including Marat and Georges Danton, blaming them for the prison massacres and the mindless bloodshed that had taken over the Revolution. Her most important subject was her own husband, who was defended and described as a virtuous man only wanting to perform his civic duty as a minister and deputy.

Women of the French Revolution

In November, Madame Roland's trial began. The prosecutor charged her with holding secret meetings, propagandizing for the Girondists, and favoring a federated republic, as opposed to the current regime controlled by the Jacobin faction. She replied to the charges, saying she was only supporting her husband in his official capacities and knew nothing of politics other than what she read in the newspapers and heard discussed in the "public conversations" held in her weekly salons.

Her cleverness with words and argument proved frustrating for her interrogators, who were determined to find her guilty of conspiring against the Revolution. As Madame Roland herself remembers the interrogation:

> The discussion was long and difficult. . . . They accused me of verbosity, and said that this wasn't the Ministry of the Interior; wit would get me nowhere. When the judge posed a question that the prosecutor didn't find to his taste, he would pose it in another manner, extending it, making it more complex, or interrupting my responses, and then requiring me to abridge them. It was a real vexation.[38]

Her eloquent words in her own defense did not save her, and on November 3 Madame Roland went to the scaffold. Soon afterward her husband committed suicide.

Ironically, illiteracy could be just as dangerous as the ability to express one's opinions in books or pamphlets. Author Carla Hesse describes the danger of illiteracy in the revolutionary years:

> Unable to read the laws now posted with unprecedented rapidity in broadside form on the streets, rather than proclaimed aloud at mass, many women of the popular classes unwittingly fell afoul of the proliferation of emergency measures.[39]

The Revolution would produce a decree establishing a system of universal public education, a measure that would go far to eliminate illiteracy among men as well as women in France. But schooling often did not reach the lowest strata of society, the rural peasants who worked the land and as children never saw the inside of a classroom. The women of this class played roles as both fighters for and determined opponents of the Revolution.

Chapter 5:
Peasants and Villagers

The peasants of France made up the bulk of the population, yet this class was far removed from the political debates fragmenting the nation in the late eighteenth century. Those who worked the land had few legal rights and very little say in how the nation was governed. For the average rural laborer, Paris was a remote, strange, chaotic cauldron of vice and corruption. The violent events of the Revolution would reinforce that view—yet the peasantry also took part in the Revolution, and several women rose from rural anonymity to play important roles in the fight.

The long, cold winter of 1788–1789 brought misery and death to the villages and farms of rural France. Rivers froze, and a thick blanket of snow covered pastures and orchards. Herds of cattle and sheep died of the cold. When the spring thaw came, the floods destroyed grain crops or made it impossible to harvest. In the meantime, starving wild animals roamed through the fields, eating seeds and young shoots.

Like peasants throughout Europe, the peasants of eighteenth-century France lived a hand-to-mouth existence. Most peasant families owned no land of their own. Instead, they rented the land they worked, paying landowners for the right to farm with an annual tribute of grain or other goods that they produced. They were often indebted to landowners for their homes as well, and most could not avoid the taxes levied by the state. The peasantry had little hope of improving their lot, as they could not afford to attend schools when young and also found artisans' guilds closed to them.

For most women of peasant households, life was a round of work, childbearing, and struggle to provide food for the rest of the family. In the best of times, these women had just enough to carry on a difficult existence. To supplement their meager income from the farm, they often took work in small factories in nearby towns or accepted raw cloth for piecework in their own homes. In times of famine, when jobs were scarce, they starved and often succumbed to illnesses such as tuberculosis, malaria, dysentery, measles, and smallpox, for which cures were unknown or treatments were beyond their means.

Madame Roland, who spent vacations in the countryside, found there escape from the turmoil of the cities—as well as poverty, disease, and hopelessness. According to author Gita May,

> Visiting the shabby hovels overcrowded with emaciated, sick human beings, she [Madame Roland] realized that, of all the French population, the peasantry was the most unfortunate and neglected. They lived in total ignorance, were treated as work animals, and yet carried the main burden of seignorial dues and governmental taxes. She saw farmers suffering from a variety of diseases, and yet continue their labor until they died without ever consulting a doctor because they could not afford the expense.[40]

Nevertheless, the peasants revered the king of France as a father and protector. They saw the king as an opponent of the wealthy landowners who weighed them down with obligations and duties. The crowning of Louis XVI brought renewed hope for a redress of the injustices that plagued them. But throughout the 1780s, taxes grew even more burdensome and crop failures forced many families to give up their farms and take to the roads to search for work in the cities, or simply to beg for food. In the spring of 1789, these frustrations reached a boiling point.

The Great Fear of 1789

The winter of 1788–1789 was one of the harshest in memory. In desperation, men and women took up arms and began killing wild game that were protected as the hunting property of nobles and landowners. The peasants ignored the game laws that punished poaching with imprisonment, fines, or death. They attacked dovecotes, from which doves and pigeons launched raids on their seed. They killed rabbits and deer that feasted on their spring crops. They paraded their kill around their villages and, if confronted by game wardens, murdered them.

Such civil disobedience grew widespread, even among the most conservative elements of the peasantry. Another form of rebellion, the attack on grain transports, was often led by women. Armed with daggers, clubs, and pitchforks, poor wives and mothers formed gangs to attack river barges and wagons loaded with grain. They seized these shipments, which were destined for warehouses near the cities, and distributed them, at a price they deemed fair, to families and local merchants. In this way, the peasantry turned its many frustrations against food hoarders and speculators who, they believed, were deliberately holding supplies off the market in order to raise prices. Simon Schama describes one such seizure:

The Liberty Cap

The French Revolution inspired a wave of patriotic fervor in people of all classes, expressed in artwork and in popular attire. Frenchwomen, in their traditional role as seamstress, produced one of the most widely recognized symbols of the conflict, the *bonnet de la liberte*, or "liberty cap," also known as the *bonnet rouge*. A soft hat made of felt, colored red, the liberty cap became a popular emblem worn by both sexes.

In Roman times, "Phrygian Caps" were worn by slaves during ceremonies in which they were given their freedom. During the American Revolution, many soldiers fighting for the colonists wore soft, red caps of felt, with the word "Liberty" sewn into the fabric. Some historians believe that the colonists adopted the cap from the voyageurs, French explorers and traders who lived along the lakes and rivers of Canada and the northern frontiers of the British colonies. The symbolic liberty cap was in turn adopted by the revolutionaries of France. The cap appeared in many allegorical paintings and engravings, and atop the head of Marianne, the female figure who still serves as a symbol of the French republic.

The best-known historical bearer of the liberty cap, however, was King Louis XVI. When a crowd of Parisians broke into the Tuileries palace on June 20, 1792, they headed directly for the king's apartments, where the king was forcefully handed a *bonnet rouge*. Fearing for his life, the king obediently placed the cap on his head; the story of this humiliation, and the king's submission to the will of the people, spread far and wide and became one of the most famous moments of the Revolution.

Frenchwomen created the liberty cap, a popular revolutionary symbol worn by both sexes.

At Viroflay it was women who set up a checkpoint on the road between Versailles and Paris, stopping convoys and searching them for grain or flour before permitting them to pass. At Jouy another attroupement of women demanded that grain be sold well below market rate and the substantial farmer of the neighborhood, a man named Bure, wisely let them have it at whatever price they asked. . . . Between March 30 and April 1 a riot at Besancon led by women enforced maximum grain prices and went on to smash up the houses of recalcitrant Parlementaires.[41]

In rural France, communication was slow, and women, nearly all illiterate, depended on rumor and word of mouth for information about events elsewhere. After the fall of the Bastille in July 1789, a "Great Fear" spread throughout the countryside. Rumors spread through cities and villages that Austrian troops were marching into France, British marines were landing on the coast, or bandits hired by the monarchy or by its supporters were roaming through the countryside, pillaging and murdering. Women hid their children in haylofts and boarded up their homes. News from Paris was sketchy, and as historian Simon Schama reports, the people in the country dreaded the prospect of a foreign invasion meant to stop the Revolution in its tracks.

Marie-Victoire Monnet, the eldest of a family of fifteen children, hid in a hayloft with three of her sisters. Their mother had provided them with a loaf of bread and a quarter of Brie, enough to sustain the siege of several days expected by the village. Brigands were already said to have slaughtered the menfolk in the immediately neighboring town. After sitting for three hours in the hot, dusty, dark barn and consuming all of the bread and cheese, the girls' terror had turned to boredom and boredom to disappointment. Marie, followed by her sisters, nervously clambered down, and with no sign of the guaranteed mayhem, returned to their house, where they found their mother and the rest of the children equally baffled by the nonappearance of the dreaded criminal element.[42]

Rumor fueled the waves of terror and hysteria that would spread across the countryside for several years after the Great Fear. The peasants felt pride at their new role as citizens in a republic of liberty and equality, but they also felt a deep anger at the Revolution's attacks on their cherished institutions, especially the church. These sentiments would

Villagers stop a carriage full of grain to beg for food. Widespread food shortages in early 1789 led some peasant women to seize grain transports.

give rise to some of the bloodiest conflicts of the revolutionary era, which took place far from the great public stage of Paris.

Hiding Revolutionary Refugees

The meeting of the Estates General, and the founding of the National Assembly, brought widespread hope for renewal and change throughout France. In the fall of 1789, soon after the nobles of the Second Estate had voluntarily abolished their feudal titles and privileges, the nationalization of church property, which was then sold at auction, offered an opportunity for peasant families to finally acquire plots of their own to farm and pass down to their heirs. In the countryside, women took part in the patriotic festivals that gathered people on village greens to raise liberty trees and acclaim the new measures that promised a betterment of their lot.

During the Revolution, many people from the cities, especially Paris, took refuge in the countryside. This flight of urban citizens grew much more important in 1792 after the capture of the Tuileries and the overthrow of the king. Many aristocrats, bourgeoisie, priests, and outspoken critics of the legislature and its measures took refuge in the barns and attics of country houses.

The women of aristocratic households saw a very different world among the villages and farms of rural France. To avoid starving in Paris, Renee-Pelagie de Montreuil, the wife of the Marquis de Sade, (who had been imprisoned since 1778 for various crimes as well as debt) fled the city in the fall of 1789, only to find herself facing new threats and dangers:

I'm in the country, not because I fear the gallows but in order not to die of hunger, and because I'm penniless. . . . My older son arrived on leave. I'm holding him on a close rein for fear that he'll fall prey to vagabonds, etc. A local butcher has been massacred. Horrors are happening that make you tremble; a few culprits have been hanged. That does not restore the dead to life. If one could stop the marauders! There are so many of them that it makes you tremble. . . . We're menaced every day with carnage. As compliant as the clergy and some of the nobility are, they're still resented. . . . When you go to bed you're never sure what's going to happen the next day.[43]

Brittany, a conservative region of northwestern France, was reputed as a safe place for opponents of the Revolution to hide, according to Marilyn Yalom:

Sympathetic Breton peasants were known to take in all sorts of people—priests, nuns, conscripts, and Vendeans on the run—despite the very real risk of being shot or imprisoned if their hidden charges were found. This was the beginning of a year during which [the aristocrat] Madame de la Rochejaquelein and her equally highborn mother lived in disguise as Breton peasants, stumbling along in their wooden shoes each morning as they went out to guard the sheep and returning at night to the farm, where they fell into bed with their clothes on.[44]

The Rise and Fall of Theroigne de Mericourt

The most famous revolutionary to rise from the peasantry was Anne-Joseph Theroigne de Mericourt. She was born in the village of Marcourt, near Belgium, in 1769. The daughter of a farmer, she was seduced by a nobleman as a teenager and later became one of the most renowned courtesans of Paris. But revolutionary fervor gripped her in

1789, when she turned with a vengeance against the nobility whose desires and pleasures she had once served. With sword in hand, she urged on the men and women storming the Bastille in July 1789 and led the crowds of market women during their march to Versailles on October 5, 1789.

During this time, Theroigne regularly went to meetings of the National Assembly to view the debates from the galleries. In 1790 she formed Les Amis de la Loi (Friends of the Law), a club reserved for men, which met in her apartment on the Rue Bouloy every Tuesday and Thursday. Her ambitions were fired by the king's announcement that he would accept the constitution, and in February she made a stirring speech to the Cordeliers club, demanding the right to take part and vote in the proceedings of the club. Although the Cordeliers applauded her words, the club members immediately passed the following resolution:

> Seeing that a canon of the Council of Macon has formally recognised that women, like men, possess a soul and an intelligence, women cannot be denied the right to make such good use of them as the previous speaker has done. Mlle Theroigne and other members of her sex will always be free to propose anything that

seems to them for the good of their country. But, as to the question of status, as to whether the Demoiselle Theroigne shall be admitted to the meeting of the District with a consultative vote, the Assembly is incompetent to take any decision; and the discussion is closed.[45]

At this time Theroigne was cutting a figure in Paris, striding through the city wearing pistols and daggers and a bright red riding habit, urging on mobs of rioters and demanding the death of aristocrats. She held a salon of her own and wrote manifestos that were posted on the walls of public buildings all over the city. According to a famous revolutionary legend, Theroigne encountered the nobleman who had seduced her during the prison massacres in Paris in September 1792. Although the noble had been condemned to death and was heading for the gallows, she would not allow him to live another minute and murdered him on the spot.

But Theroigne had enemies among the market women and Jacobin faction. When she protested against the women who guarded the Assembly doors, and who regularly beat up Jacobin enemies, she became their target. On May 15, 1793, while she was walking to the Assembly, a mob of angry women attacked her and beat her senseless. She

The Revolutionary Calendar

❦

Revolutionaries hailed their era as the dawning of a new age in which all aspects of daily life, even the traditional Gregorian calendar, would be transformed. Devised by Philippe Fabre d'Eglantine, a new calendar was adopted by the National Convention in October 1793, and the people of France were instructed to observe it immediately.

According to the revolutionary calendar, Year 1 began in September 1792. The year consisted of twelve months of thirty days. Each month consisted of three weeks of ten days, with the final day of each week considered a day of rest and reflection. The five extra days of the year were dubbed the *sans-culottides*, or holidays of the sansculottes, and added to the end of the year. The five days of the *sans-culottides* were dedicated to Genius, Labor, Noble Actions, Awards, and Opinion; the sixth *sans-culottide* of the leap year, which took place every four years, was dedicated to the Revolution. The revolutionary year officially began on 1 Vendemaire, or what had once been known as September 22. The months were grouped into four seasons:

Autumn: Vendemaire (vintage), Brumaire (mist), Frimaire (frost)

Winter: Nivose (snow), Pluviose (rain), Ventose (wind)

Spring: Germinal (seed), Floreal (blossom), Prairal (meadow)

Summer: Messidor (harvest), Thermidor (heat), Fructidor (fruit)

The revolutionary calendar remained in use until abandoned by a decree of Napoléon Bonaparte on January 1, 1806.

slowly lost her reason and, although she survived the Revolution, spent the next twenty-three years of her life in asylums.

A Declaration of the Rights of Woman

The decline of Theroigne de Mericourt coincided with the rise to fame of a butcher's daughter, Marie Gouze. Married at the age of sixteen and widowed just a few years later, Marie Gouze took her mother's middle name of Olympe, changed her surname to Gouges, and adopted the aristocratic "de" to place herself, at least by the appearance of her name, in a higher social class. Instead of marrying again, as was expected, Olympe de Gouges devoted

Anne-Joseph Theroigne de Mericourt walked the streets of Paris wearing pistols and daggers and called for death to the nobility.

tion of the Rights of Woman and the Female Citizen in 1791, dedicating this document to Queen Marie-Antoinette. The seventeen articles of her declaration demanded that the laws apply equally to men and women; that women hold an equal place in society according to their talents and abilities; that the government allow freedom of public speech and written expression; and that property be held by either gender according to their legal claim to it. In a postscript to the declaration, she wrote:

Woman, wake up; the tocsin of reason is being heard throughout the whole universe; discover your rights. The powerful empire of nature is no longer surrounded by prejudice, fanaticism, superstition, and lies. The flame of truth has dispersed all the clouds of folly and usurpation. Enslaved man has multiplied his strength and needs recourse to yours to break his chains. Having become free, he has become unjust to his companion. Oh, wom-

herself to the Revolution and the cause of women's rights. She spoke out for a new divorce law, for the elimination of slavery, and for the establishment of a women's theater and new hospitals for expectant mothers.

In imitation of the Declaration of the Rights of Man and of the Citizen, Olympe de Gouges wrote the Declara-

Women of the French Revolution

en, women! When will you cease to be blind?[46]

De Gouges, who saw France's best hope in a constitutional monarchy, supported the king and queen and believed that a new equality for women would strengthen the king's authority. A supporter of the Girondists, she found herself in danger as the Girondists were suppressed in the spring of 1793. Nevertheless, she remained an outspoken critic of the Convention and the radical Jacobins. Later in the year, she was condemned for writing proclamations that supported a federalist system (a system of decentralized power, as opposed to the rule imposed on the nation from Paris by the Jacobins). The charges against her showed how certain opinions had become capital crimes in revolutionary France:

From the examination of the documents deposited, together with the interrogation of the accused, it follows that against the desire manifested by the majority of Frenchmen for republican government, and in contempt of laws directed against whoever might propose another form of government, Olympe de Gouges composed and had printed works which can only be considered as an attack on the sovereignty of the people.... The author of this work openly provoked civil war and sought to arm citizens against one another.[47]

The tribunal agreed and found de Gouges too sympathetic to the monarchy and to a federal form of government. On November 3, 1793, she died on the guillotine, while pleading for her life—in vain—by claiming that she was pregnant.

After the death of Olympe de Gouges, the deputy Anaxagore Chaumette pointed her out as a lesson to other women who would presume to meddle in political affairs, which were properly the domain of men: "Remember that virago, that woman-man, the impudent Olympe de Gouges, who abandoned all the cares of her household because she wanted to engage in politics and commit crimes.... This forgetfulness of the virtues of her sex led her to the scaffold."[48]

The Peasant Revolt in the Vendée

The rabid attack by the Jacobins on the monarchy and the church, symbols held dear by the peasants for many generations, changed the perception of the Revolution for the worse in rural France. Women played a prominent role in peasant uprisings in Brittany, in the mountains of the Massif Central, and in rural Provence in southeastern France. Devoted churchgoers, peasant women also led many demonstrations against new constitutional clergy—priests who had sworn to support the new constitution and who were sent to replace "refractory" priests who would not swear this oath. Many women set up chapels and altars within their homes, to which they would invite the refractory priests barred by the revolutionary

The Cockade

The revolutionary *cocarde* (cockade) was a small badge or ribbon worn by supporters of the Revolution. It originated in a small cockade of red and blue worn by the Paris militia during the demonstrations of the summer of 1789. Later, the Marquis de Lafayette, the commander of the National Guard, ordered the color white to be added to the cockade. White was the ancient color of the Bourbon monarchy, and Lafayette's innovation symbolized the reconciliation of the king and his people. The *tricolore* (three-colored) cockade, displayed on hats or clothing, became an all but obligatory emblem of "correct" political allegiance. In imitation, rival factions such as the aristocracy created their own cockades (the aristocratic cockade was pure white or black), but few dared to wear them in public.

On February 15, 1794, the French Assembly officially adopted the *tricolore* as the flag of the new republic. On a recommendation from the painter Jacques-Louis David, the law stated that the cockade would show vertical stripes of blue, white, and red, with blue lying closest to the flagstaff.

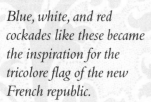
Blue, white, and red cockades like these became the inspiration for the tricolore flag of the new French republic.

Women of the French Revolution

authorities from performing mass. Women formed large crowds to harass and ridicule the constitutional priests; they left garbage and unburied corpses at the church doors for the intruders to clean up; and they stayed away from Sunday mass by the millions. They also refused to take part in civil marriage ceremonies, to attend funerals, or to allow their newborns to be baptized by constitutional priests. One such priest from Paris, installed in the Church of Le May-sur-Evre, found women following him into his church and making a display of cleaning away his "polluting" footprints from the floor.

In the Vendée, a poor and isolated rural region of western France, the peasantry remained steadfastly loyal to the monarchy throughout the Revolution. In the spring of 1793, soon after the execution of Louis XVI, the men and women of this region rose up in revolt. The spark that set off this insurrection was a decree of February 24 in which the Convention ordered the conscription of 300,000 men to defend the Revolution against its foreign enemies. By the thousands, women left their homes to join the small armies that were marching against the towns, determined to attack National Guard units as well as revolutionary officials and mayors. In response the Convention ordered the destruction of the Vendée. Republican armies marched on the region, ravaging the countryside and killing thousands of peasants.

Peasant women took part in this uprising not only as fighters but as non-combatants. They provided safe houses for Vendean soldiers in flight from the republican armies. They carried messages, sewed clothing, dressed wounds, supplied bread and water, and ambushed isolated units or solitary enemy soldiers.

In the Vendée and the rest of France, similar small civil wars left the peasantry destitute, as battles and conscription disrupted the raising of crops and livestock. Under the Directory that followed the Revolution, rural life slowly returned to its normal occupations and seasonal rhythms. The women of French farms and villages saw some improvement in their lives, including better opportunities for education and more jobs available to them, should they choose to move away, in town and city workshops. In the meantime, traditions held dear under the Old Regime, including attendance at Sunday mass and devotion to the church and clergy, returned as if never disrupted by the years of revolutionary frenzy.

Chapter 6:
Women and Religion

The Catholic Church was a wealthy and powerful institution in prerevolutionary France. The church owned extensive land and thousands of productive estates; its members enjoyed exemption from taxes, military service, and other obligations to the king. All members of society revered the church and held to its teachings, despite the skepticism of Enlightenment philosophers who saw church doctrine as superstitious dogma. Women, in particular, accepted Christian beliefs and made up a majority of those who celebrated the Catholic mass. Though barred from the priesthood, many women took holy vows as nuns and many more were educated in religious schools. The power and the wealth of the church, however, did not protect churchwomen from the furies of the Revolution, which brought drastic changes, and near destruction, to the French Catholic Church.

Catholicism in France

France on the eve of the Revolution was a Catholic country. The kingdom had resisted the Protestant Reformation and reserved full legal rights for its Catholic citizens. The peasantry and middle classes felt a strong devotion to the church and regularly attended Sunday mass. Their local parish priest performed the sacraments: baptism, marriage, and extreme unction, the rite performed for the dying. The priest also drew up the parish register, a list of all baptized members of a community. In this way, church membership conferred normal civil status on the people.

Yet the nation was not uniformly religious. The people of certain regions of France were fiercely loyal to the church and to the pope, the earthly head of the church, who resided in Rome. In the countryside, the people largely accepted and followed traditional Catholic teachings. But those in the port cities and the boundary regions, more open to the influence of foreign beliefs and societies, tended to drift from church practices and beliefs. The large cities, also, were home to religious skepticism. Historians have also pointed out a difference in the religious practices of men and women. In her essay "De-Christianization," author Mona Ozouf explains:

> A disparity between male and female observance (invariably an indication of declining practice overall) had begun in rural central France. Necker had already noticed that men were likely to leave church before the sermon and return just in time for the consecration, a practice that would become common in the nineteenth century.[49]

Though women were barred from the clergy, they could join the church as nuns. Many entered convents out of religious devotion. Some sought escape from personal or family turmoil or simply for a respectable, secure role in the absence of offers of marriage. Taking perpetual vows of chastity, obedience,

This tableau in a French museum depicts nuns like those in Revolutionary France. Frenchwomen became nuns for many reasons, including religious devotion, to escape turmoil, or because they had no offers of marriage.

and poverty, nuns wore distinctive habits (uniforms) and moved into small, enclosed communities of the devout. In some convents, they instructed the daughters of the nobility and middle classes in the catechism and the rituals of worship.

Other women joined the Order of Hospitalieres, which dated to the medieval Crusades. In cities throughout France, the women of this order lived and worked in the local *Hotel-Dieu* or *Maison-Dieu*, the House of God. They took monastic vows, but instead of removing themselves from society, they cared for the sick and injured or attended to foundlings and orphans. At the time of the Revolution, the Hotel-Dieu of Paris was the order's largest and best-known establishment. Located on the Ile de la Cité, the island in the Seine River on which Notre Dame cathedral stood, the Hotel-Dieu accommodated three thousand patients.

Dismantling Religious Orders

The good works of religious orders did not persuade France's revolutionaries to spare the church from sweeping new laws. On August 4, 1789, the National Assembly abolished all church privileges as well as the tithe (taxes levied for the benefit of the church). On November 2, the Assembly confiscated all church property—which constituted 10 percent of all land in the kingdom—in order to pay off the nation's debts. That fall, the Assembly also abolished monastic vows, seeing them as a relic of feudalism and as contrary to the principle of individual liberty. By a decree of February 13, 1790, all religious orders, except for teaching or hospital orders, were abolished. Many monasteries and convents were closed down by force, their properties seized and sold off to the highest bidders.

The banning of vows and monastic orders released nuns from their obligations. Many nuns, however, did not want to return to society at large. In the spring of 1790, government representatives arrived at the doors of convents all over France to take inventories of land and goods and to receive the declaration of the nuns as to whether they would stay or leave. John McManners, in *The French Revolution and the Church*, describes the reluctance of many women to abandon their vows and convents:

The vast majority of nuns remained loyal to their vocation—in startling contrast to monks, who in large numbers seized the chance of freedom. There are some obvious practical reasons for this sharp statistical contrast. Male and female religious were to be treated very differently; the former were to be moved off in huddles into a few selected institu-

A contemporary sketch depicts revolutionaries evicting clerics from their church. A decree of early 1790 abolished all religious orders in France.

tions, the latter were to stay in their own houses and in their own order. Most houses of women did some sort of educational or charitable work. . . . It was harder, too, for women to venture out into the world and start life again. There was no place in society as yet for the independent unmarried woman.[50]

The Civil Constitution of the Clergy was passed on July 12, 1790. On November 26, members of the clergy were ordered to swear an oath to the new constitution. If they did not, they were liable to prosecution for disturbing the peace. This new decree split the church into two factions: the "constitutional" clergy, who swore to uphold the Revolution, and the "refractory" clergy, who refused to take the oath and who remained faithful to the pope, the head of the Catholic Church. According to the proclamations of the pope, only those weddings and baptisms conducted by refractory priests were still blessed by the church.

The old calendar, including the traditional Christian holidays and saints' days, was banished in favor of a new revolutionary calendar. The mass of the *decadi*, which occurred every tenth day, replaced traditional Sunday mass. The new mass celebrated the cult of the

Life in the Cloister

❦

One of the most important functions of the convents of eighteenth-century France was the education of young girls, who were barred from attendance at French universities. But as was in the rest of French society, religious education was organized along class lines. In the city of Angers, for example, three religious houses accepted young women as boarders and pupils: the Visitation, a house for the daughters of the rich; the Ursulines, which accepted middle-class girls; and La Providence, a home for orphans, runaways, and unemployed servant girls.

In the convent, girls were educated not only in religious studies and catechism but also in the social graces: dancing, singing, and etiquette. In some religious houses, they were also trained as teachers or in the care of the sick. All convents imposed strict rules of appearance and behavior: As boarders, young girls had to give up the vanities of the ordinary world, including hair curls, face powder, fashionable clothes, card playing, and the reading of novels.

nation, which had its origins in the Festival of the Federation that took place in 1790. Even minor habits of religious faith were condemned, according to McManners:

> Many women . . . found it difficult to relinquish the habit of crossing themselves. One newspaper recommended that those who could not cure themselves of this superstitious practice might at least render it innocuous by mumbling as they made the sign, instead of the traditional phrase "in the name of the Father, Son, and Holy Ghost," the words "in the name of my country, liberty, and equality."[51]

Adherence to Religious Practice

Despite this campaign against the church and its clergy, millions of ordinary Frenchwomen remained devoted churchgoers. If their churches closed, they continued their devotions in private homes, sometimes under the direction of refractory priests who had to practice their faith in secret. Historian Stanley Loomis describes a sixteen-year-old named Louise Gely, the daughter of a clerk:

> Louise . . . was a woman educated in the spirit of religious principles . . . an uncomplicated creature whose

behaviour was governed by the concerns traditional to most respectable French housewives: family, God, and domestic economy. . . . More than this, however, Louise and her family had remained practicing Catholics throughout the religious persecutions that had begun with Marat's ascendancy to power. This means that they made their confession to and received the sacraments from the hands of a priest who had not sworn an oath to the Constitution. Such men were of course outlaws, as were the men and women who received their ministrations, and all were liable to the death penalty.[52]

In June 1793, Louise Gely married Georges-Jacques Danton, a leading Jacobin and a radical firebrand of the Revolution. She had convinced Danton to make a full confession to a refractory abbot, the Abbe Kerenavent, and marry her in a traditional church ceremony. The influence of his young and deeply religious wife, in the eyes of many historians, softened Danton's enthusiasm for a revolution that was every day turning more violent.

De-Christianization Intensifies

In November 1793, under the direction of Maximilien Robespierre and his Committee of Public Safety, the Convention passed a decree that forbade all churches in Paris from practicing traditional Catholic worship. In the meantime, the Jacobin faction, now in control of the Revolution, decreed the "de-Christianization" of France. Government representatives sent from Paris coordinated an all-out campaign against the church and the symbols of Christianity. Revolutionary militants raided churches all over France, smashing statues and other images of Christ and the saints, pillaging cemeteries, looting altars of their silver and gold objects, and seizing bronze church bells to be melted down for bullets. Priests took part in forced marriage ceremonies, and nuns were turned out of their convents and in some places attacked, raped, and murdered. The pope was burned in effigy, and in many villages the people made bonfires from priestly vestments, crucifixes, Bibles, and statues. Animals were dressed in the robes of bishops and paraded through the streets to the laughter and ridicule of bystanders.

The Marquis de Sade, a notoriously immoral author of erotic novels, joined in the insults and desecration of the church. Proclaiming the rise of a new feminine symbol of the nation's faith, he wrote:

> Man is finally enlightened. . . . Reason takes the place of Mary in our hearts, and the incense that used to burn to an adulterous woman will

A sketch depicts a parade of the Goddess of Reason through the streets of Paris. As France was de-Christianized, a new religion, the cult of Supreme Reason, took hold.

from now on be lit only at the feet of that Goddess [Reason] which severed our chains. . . . Let symbols of morality be placed, in each church, upon the same altar where vain vows used to be pledged to a chimera. Let these emblems, while firing our hearts, make us pass from idolatry to wisdom; let filial piety, greatness of soul, courage, equality, good faith, love of the fatherland . . . let all these virtues, erected in each of our ancient temples, become the only objects of our veneration.[53]

In Paris, a new religion—the cult of Supreme Reason, later the cult of the Supreme Being—was officially dedicated at the cathedral of Notre Dame. The ancient seat of French Catholicism had been closed to worship since 1790. The statues within the cathedral had been destroyed, the lead from the coffins of the archbishops of Paris torn away and melted down for bullets, the tombs of the kings of France opened, and the

Women of the French Revolution

ashes of the dead rulers, symbols of a bygone tyranny, scattered in the air. At one point, the authorities considered tearing down the cathedral entirely.

Instead, on November 10, Notre Dame was rechristened the Temple of Reason. At this ceremony, an opera singer, the "Citizeness Aubry," appeared as the Goddess of Reason. Using sets from the Opera of Paris, the republicans raised an ancient pagan temple to replace the Christian altar, as well as a statue of Liberty, a female figure. On a throne at the entrance to the temple sat Mademoiselle Aubry, posing as the goddess Reason, dressed in a white robe and the red liberty cap and holding a pikestaff in her hands. As Aubry bowed to a flame of Reason, a chorus of young girls sang a hymn to Liberty. Similar festivals of Reason took place in cathedrals throughout France, with actresses personifying the new ideals of the republic just as female figures represented the nation in engravings, statuary, and paintings created to celebrate the new republic.

Prophets and Mystics

As the traditional church disappeared from view, many women turned to private cults of seers. One such prophet, Suzette Labrousse, had said in 1779 that the clergy of France would lose their property, a prediction that came true in 1789. At the outbreak of the Revolu-tion, she walked from her home in the Dordogne region three hundred miles to Paris, where she was received by the duchess of Bourbon, an aristocratic woman who brought religious mystics

Rose Philippine Duchesne

Among the survivors of the French Revolution, Rose Philippine Duchesne made the most significant mark on religious life in the New World. She was born in 1769 to a wealthy family of Grenoble, in southeastern France. She took up the life of a nun after refusing to marry a man selected for her by her father. After the outbreak of the Revolution, Duchesne organized the Ladies of Mercy, a group of women who remained loyal to the church and who brought help to the sick and poor, sometimes at great risk of arrest by the revolutionary authorities. After the Revolution, she helped establish new convent schools in France and Belgium, and in 1818 she sailed to the New World. She founded the first Sacred Heart convent in St. Joseph, Missouri, then on the frontier, the first such school for poor girls west of the Mississippi River. Duchesne died in 1852 and was canonized in 1988.

and fanatics into her circle of friends. In 1792 Labrousse was invited by seven constitutional bishops to appear before them and give an example of her powers. According to Winifred Stephens, "She predicted the resurrection of the Dauphin, Louis XVI's eldest son, who had died at the beginning of the Revolution, and of Mirabeau. On being asked when the resurrections would take place, she replied, 'Soon.' When urged to be more explicit, she was wisely silent. On the inquiry as to whether it would be within three or four months, she equivocally nodded her head."[54]

Impressed, the bishops appointed Labrousse as their representative to the pope in Rome. She was to gain his blessing for the Revolution and the Constitution of the Clergy. But when she reached the Italian city of Bologna, she was driven away by representatives of the pope. She was arrested soon afterward and imprisoned in the Castel St. Angelo, an ancient Roman fortress, for six years. When French troops seized Rome in 1798, she finally won her freedom. But when she returned to France in 1799—when she had already predicted the world would come to an end—she found that few people took an interest in her prophecies.

Another famous revolutionary-era mystic was Catherine Theot, a former nun of fanatical religious devotion. Theot held regular séances in her apartment on the Rue Contrescarpe in Paris. Believers from all over the city came to receive her blessings and to be initiated into her secret rites. The sick came to be cured, and soldiers came for protection before marching to the battlefront. Theot held the Revolution to be an act of God and condemned all refractory priests as enemies of the new religion.

During the Reign of Terror, Theot became an ally of Robespierre, the head of the Committee of Public Safety who was sending innocent citizens to the guillotine by the hundreds. Theot hailed Robespierre as a man of virtue and as the savior of France. In June 1794, the police raided her home and discovered a letter, which may have been planted, in which she hailed Robespierre as her son and as France's new Messiah. Theot was arrested on the orders of Marc Guillaume Vadier, a rival of Robespierre, and thrown in prison. Vadier brought Theot's letter to the Convention and used it to ridicule Robespierre before the representatives, an action that encouraged resistance to the Reign of Terror. Theot remained in prison through the coup of July 27, when Robespierre was overthrown, and she died there two months later.

Martyrs to the Faith

Despite the official closing of their convents and the banning of religious vows, many nuns continued their religious observances in secret. By doing so, they risked their lives. In the summer of 1794, sixteen nuns of the Carmelite order in the town of Compiegne were arrested and brought to trial. All were found guilty of treason to the Revolution, condemned to death, and brought to Paris for their execution. On July 17, the appointed day, they were bundled into the death carts. Their slow journey to the execution ground was famously dramatic: During the entire journey, the condemned women sang with great dignity a solemn hymn known as the *Miserere*. The haunting sound silenced the crowds that watched their tumbrels pass. Reaching the base of the scaffold, their prioress held a small terra-cotta statue of the Madonna and Jesus. Each sister kissed the statue, requested permission to die from their mother superior, and mounted the steps to the guillotine.

Rather than jeering at the condemned, the crowds that gathered to witness the execution of the Carmelite nuns were unusually silent. For a year the Terror had brought bloodshed and treachery to Paris and the rest of France, as thousands were condemned and put to death on the word of neighbors, rivals, and the Committee of Public Safety. Many historians believe that the devotion and courage of the nuns inspired the opposition that finally broke

Maximilien Robespierre and ended his Reign of Terror. One week after the mass execution, Robespierre was overthrown and sent to the scaffold himself.

With the death of Robespierre, a new government was established. A reaction against the symbols and excesses of the Revolution took place. Many Frenchwomen returned to the church and to regular Sunday mass, and refractory priests came out of their hiding places. But French society was still divided into bitterly opposed factions, and violence had become commonplace. The execution of those considered opponents of the Revolution continued, as the conflict reached the most popular religious orders and the most sheltered and devout women of the church.

One such group, the Order of St. Ursula, had originated in sixteenth-century Italy. The order was established for the purpose of educating young girls. From Italy the order spread to Germany and France, and it had established several hundred monasteries throughout France by the time of the Revolution. The nuns of this order, named for a fifth-century Christian woman martyred by the Huns, dedicated themselves completely to teaching. French families by the thousands sent their daughters to Ursuline convents for their education.

When the revolutionary government closed the Ursuline school and convent at

Maximilien Robespierre is led to the guillotine in 1794. Robespierre was executed shortly after he executed sixteen Carmelite nuns as part of his Reign of Terror.

Valenciennes, in northern France, the nuns moved to another convent in Mons, in the territory of Belgium, then controlled by the Austrian emperor. By the laws of the Revolution, this act made them émigrés and traitors to the nation. In 1793 Austrian troops crossed the border and seized Valenciennes. The nuns returned to their former home, but when the French troops recaptured Valenciennes, the nuns were arrested and thrown into prison for illegally returning to France after emigrating. On October 17, 1794, five of the nuns were put on trial, sentenced to death, and led to the guillotine. Five days later, when the mother superior of the community, Marie Clotilde Paillot, and five more nuns were

Women of the French Revolution

being brought to their execution, a lay sister of the Ursulines, Cordule Barre, jumped in the cart of her own free will to be executed with the rest. In 1920 the Ursuline martyrs of Valenciennes were beatified by Pope Benedict XV.

The Revolution's war on the church abated after this event. Nevertheless, the religious life of France had been permanently transformed. Parish registers were replaced by civil registers, kept by the secular authorities. Marriages had to be first registered and recognized at the local city hall, while religious weddings became optional for all. Members of the church, including nuns, had the legal authority to marry, if they wished. And in the view of Mona Ozouf, the Revolution also caused a sharp decline in religious observance by the common people:

> If de-Christianization means a decline of religious practice, again

the results were dramatic. The Revolution aggravated existing differences in religious observance by men and women, hastened male abstinence from Easter communion, and inaugurated the two antagonistic centers of village social life of the nineteenth century, the church for women and the tavern for men.[55]

By the Law of Ventose, passed in 1795, the ban on public worship was ended, and by another law passed on March 30, 1795, fifteen Catholic churches were officially reopened. This law signaled the slow restoration of church institutions, including monasteries and convents. While some women returned to their convents, others stayed outside the church, to become teachers or join the workforce in a drastically changed French society.

Chapter 7:
Women Soldiers

The armies of France, as in the rest of Europe, had always been a strictly male reserve. Under the Bourbon kings, only men were subject to conscription levies in wartime, and only men served the king as officers. There were a few examples of women who hid their gender to volunteer and fight, often for the sake of joining their husbands, sons, or brothers in the field. But since the campaigns of Joan of Arc in the fifteenth century, no woman had distinguished herself as a French military hero.

In many ways the Revolution drastically changed the role and the rights of women in French society. The legal right to bear arms and fight in uniform, however, was still denied them. Many female leaders protested this ban, and many women defied the restrictions on military service to take up arms and join the fight. In a plea for the right to bear arms for the Revolution, an author in the revolutionary journal *Mere Duchesne* proclaimed in 1791:

I offer my services to the nation as a warrior. I am naturally inclined to fist fight, and I am used to boxing with my dear husband. At the first drumbeat I take up arms, I raise a squadron of Amazons, I put myself at their head, I thrust into the enemy battalions as if they were butter.[56]

The Formation of Volunteer Battalions

The coming of the Revolution brought requests from several women's political clubs for the arming of battalions of female volunteers for the defense of the Revolution. In Paris several such units formed, with women marching and drilling with swords and pikes, weapons that were easily available to them. None of these units were ever permitted to take the field, however, prompting leaders such as Pauline Leon to make more formal demands. On March 6, 1791, two years before founding the Society of Revolutionary Republican Women, Leon rose to speak before the National Assembly. She presented a petition to the legislators to grant women the right to bear arms, and proclaimed:

> Patriotic women come before you to claim the right which any individual has to defend his life and liberty. . . . Yes, Gentlemen, we need arms, and we come to ask your permission to procure them. May our weakness be no obstacle; courage and intrepidity will supplant it, and the love of the fatherland and hatred of tyrants will allow us to brave all dangers with ease. . . . You cannot refuse us, and society cannot deny the right nature gives us, unless you pretend the Declaration of Rights does not apply to women, and that they should let their throats be cut like lambs, without the right to defend themselves.[57]

Leon asked the Assembly to grant permission for women to obtain and use pistols and muskets, to assemble regularly in the open for training in the use of these arms, and to place themselves

In defense of the Revolution, many women took up arms and formed volunteer battalions. However, they were denied the legal right to participate in the military.

under the command of officers of the National Guard. But this petition and all similar petitions were ignored, with little debate. The male leaders of the Revolution still had traditional notions of a woman's proper place as being in the home, supporting and sustaining her husband and family. They were not ready to allow women to fight, and many of them looked on all such women's petitions as laughable diversions from more serious business.

This did not discourage Leon and other female leaders, including Olympe de Gouges, from making a show of their determination to fight for the Revolution. During a Festival of the Federation in 1792, de Gouges took command of a company of armed women. In one of her pamphlets, she argued that women should organize an armed bodyguard to protect the queen. Although this idea never came to pass, women devoted to Maximilien Robespierre did form such a bodyguard to protect him from assassins.

Joining the Regular Army

Women determined to actually take up arms and fight did not bother with ceremonial marches or petitions to the Assembly. Historians estimate that there were several hundred women, the vast majority whose names are unknown, who fought in the armies of the repub-

lic and among the royalist forces fighting against the Revolution. These female soldiers simply presented themselves at hastily assembled conscription centers, where physical examinations were short and careless. They cut their hair short and wore trousers to deceive the recruiters, and the army issued them uniforms, weapons, and ammunition. Although most had to march, fight, and sleep in disguise, in some instances they remained in their units with the support of male commanding officers.

Civilian women also followed the armies to serve as cooks, laundresses, and servants. In his book *The Soldiers of the French Revolution*, historian Alan Forrest writes of the many prostitutes who also attached themselves to military units:

The political leaders might speak in high moral tones of the damage caused to French fighting strength by the "plague" of prostitutes that followed the armies. The Convention even tried to clean up the camps in April 1793: "useless" women were to be sent home immediately, including soldiers' wives who were given 5 sous per mile to see them on their way. Battalions were limited to four laundresses to wash the men's linen. But such draconian measures had little effect on the ground. In practice, the armies tolerated the presence of prostitutes and camp followers . . . and when controls were introduced to restrain the gaggles of women who were such a feature of garrison towns, these controls were generally motivated by fear of disease rather than by any puritanical revolutionary concern for morality.[58]

The Fernig Sisters

The bravery of two well-known revolutionary warriors, the Fernig sisters, inspired the Parisian Manette Dupont to organize a battalion of nine hundred women. The women prepared to disguise themselves as men and march to the frontiers, as Dupont asked the Convention to organize a "Fernig Regiment" of ten thousand female warriors. Her request was refused, and Dupont's women's battalion never marched, but the legend of the Fernig sisters lived on.

In the territory of Alsace, in eastern France, a nobleman named Louis Joseph de Fernig had been living a quiet life after serving with distinction in the Seven Years' War (1755–1762). A lover of books and philosophy, he was a personal friend of the Enlightenment philosopher Voltaire. His two daughters, Felicite (born in 1776) and Theophile (born in 1779), were not content with living indoors, however, as proper aristocratic women did. They spent their days riding through the countryside, training

A New Kind of Punishment

An old custom of the French army came under attack by women fighting for their rights and their recognition during the Revolution. As a result, an anonymous "Ladies' Request to the National Assembly," quoted in Karen Offen's *European Feminisms, 1700–1795*, made the following proposal:

> When a soldier has, out of cowardice, compromised French honor, he will no longer be degraded as is the present custom, by making him wear women's clothing; but as the two sexes are and must be equally honorable in the eyes of humanity, he will henceforth be punished by declaring his gender to be neuter.

themselves to fight and shoot.

When the Revolution broke out, Fernig became a commander of the National Guard, the army formed to defend the Revolution from its enemies both within and outside France. When he returned home from one of his campaigns against the Austrians, his tales of battle and suffering inspired his daughters. When they heard about the defeat of the French at Longwy in September

Women Soldiers

1792, the girls put on uniforms brought home by their elder brother and, without telling their father, joined Louis de Fernig's company at the battlefront.

Inspired by stories of bravery and battle, Felicite (left) and Theophile de Fernig donned men's clothing and joined the revolutionary army.

When a high-ranking officer of the republican army arrived one day to inspect Fernig's company, the daughters' high-pitched voices quickly gave them away. Proud of the surprising discovery, Fernig allowed his daughters to remain in the army, and General Charles Dumouriez, overall commander of the republican army, made the Fernig sisters his personal aides. Through the winter and spring, they took part in four major battles. The male soldiers who marched and fought beside them viewed them as lucky signs of victory and spread tales of their incredible exploits. According to author Winifred Stephens:

[The general] loved to tell of the courage they displayed on more than one occasion . . . how Theophile, in an engagement near Brussels, when an enemy officer summoned her to surrender, with one pistol shot stretched him at her feet; how at Jemappes, when, with a handful of horsemen, she was attacking a Hungarian battalion, with her own hand she took prisoner and disarmed the most formidable of the grenadiers. . . . But Dumouriez's favorite story was of Theophile's capture of a huge Austrian whom she led to the Commander-in-Chief, saying in her girlish treble, "General, here is a prisoner I have brought you." The piping voice staggered the Austrian, who was furious to find that he had surrendered to a girl.[59]

The Fernig sisters felt their strongest loyalty to General Dumouriez. But Dumouriez found himself in an impossible situation when the Jacobin leaders, suspecting his loyalty to them, refused to send arms to the front. When the general went over to the Austrians, the Fernig sisters followed him. The Convention, which had often praised and proclaimed their deeds, immediately condemned the Fernig sisters as traitors and émigrés. The betrayal of the Fernig sisters inspired the Convention to officially ban women from the army, either as camp followers or as soldiers, in the spring of 1793. All these women discovered in the ranks were granted safe-conduct passports and were paid a small sum to return to their homes.

Capitaine Dubois at the Siege of Maastricht

In early 1793, while the Fernig sisters were fighting with General Dumouriez, Elizabeth Francois Dubois donned male clothing and presented herself to a recruiter. She joined her husband, Cap-

The Committee of Public Safety Calls the Nation to Service

Threatened by an invasion of foreign armies seeking to overthrow the Revolution, the Committee of Public Safety announced a mass conscription on August 23, 1793. Historians often mark this levee en masse as the first time that all citizens of a nation—men, women, and children—were mobilized for war. But the proclamation set out specific roles and duties for each gender, as quoted on the Modern History Sourcebook Web site:

From this moment until that in which the enemy shall have been driven from the soil of the Republic, all Frenchmen are in permanent requisition for the service of the armies. The young men shall go to battle; the married men shall forge arms and transport provisions; the women shall make tents and clothing and shall serve in the hospitals; the children shall turn old linen into lint; the aged shall betake themselves to the public places in order to arouse the courage of the warriors and preach the hatred of kings and the unity of the Republic.

tain Pierre Louis Favre of the Seventh Battalion artillery, at Liege on February 11 and put on the uniform of a *capitaine*. Five days later, she began marching with him against the counterrevolutionary armies of Austria. On February 22, the company joined the siege of Maastricht, in what is now the Netherlands, and Dubois had her first taste of battle. As she later testified, the army and its gunners were woefully unprepared:

> Because the shot and shells were not up to caliber, [we] were reduced to shooting only twelve times a day. The munitions were so poorly supplied that there were no cartridge boxes ready; there was not a single

A contemporary painting depicts the 1794 siege of Maastricht in what is now the Netherlands. The republican army of France was soundly defeated because it was unprepared and undersupplied.

Women of the French Revolution

twenty-four pounder [heavy cannon] mounted when the attack began, and there were different-caliber shot mixed pell-mell, so it was necessary to sort them out. When there were shot, there was no powder; and when someone had powder, he lacked shot and there was no fire grate ready for use. . . . The moment the order for lifting the siege arrived, the whole army was lost in tears of despair.[60]

The lifting of the siege of Maastricht resulted in a rout. The republican army fled, and Dubois was captured by the Austrians. Her captors took her money and uniform and threw her into the dungeon of Tirlemont, where the Austrian guards were methodically slaughtering the prisoners with swords and bayonets. Just before her execution, her captors pulled off her vest and discovered that she was a woman. The enemy commander sent her to another prison, where she steadfastly refused to give away passwords or any other information under interrogation. In the meantime, she listened closely to the conversations of the officers, who did not realize she understood German. When she was freed, Dubois returned to Paris and gave a report on enemy strategy and the schemes of French émigrés, who were informing the Austrians of the republi-

can plans and encouraging the enemy to massacre republican fighters.

The Vendée Uprising

Meanwhile, in the Vendée region, a very different war was taking place between the local population and republican armies sent to put down a counterrevolutionary uprising. Outraged by a demand of the Convention for conscripts to fight at the borders, the people of Vendée rose up in revolt in March 1793. Vendean peasants and townspeople murdered hundreds of republican officials and formed brigades of volunteers to fight with muskets, pikes, and pitchforks. In the village of Doulon, one proclamation read, "They have killed our king; chased away our priests; sold the goods of our church; eaten everything we have and now they want to take our bodies. . . . No, they shall not have them."[61]

Women played a vital role in the Vendée insurrection. There were few rules about who could or could not fight, and women dressed as men had little trouble finding acceptance in the rebel brigades. Some joined the companies on foot, while others rode their own horses into battle. Many women served the uprising as messengers, nurses, and supply carriers, who brought clothing and ammunition from place to place. One noblewoman, Mademoiselle

Tome I.er page 412

RENÉE BORDEREAU *dite* L'ANGEVIN,
Cavalier Vendéen,
Née à Soulaine près d'Angers, en Juin 1770.

Renee Bordereau's valor in battle inspired the men of the Vendean army to fight with greater courage.

I saw two sisters, fourteen and fifteen years old, who were very courageous. In the army of Dr. Bonchamp, a young woman became a dragoon to avenge the death of her father, and performed prodigious feats of valor during the whole war, under the name *L'angevine.* I one day saw a young woman, tall and beautiful, with pistols and a saber hung at her girdle, come to Chollet, accompanied by two other women armed with pikes. She told me that she was from the parish of Tout-Le-Monde, and that the women kept guard there when the men were absent in the army.[62]

Renee Bordereau

The Vendean fighter known to Madame de la Rochejaquelein as *L'angevine* was Renee Bordereau, who joined the rebellion after experiencing the worst that war has to offer. Said Bordereau:

The insurrection of the royalists in the Vendée, in 1793, brought to our country armies of republicans who

de la Rochefoucault, took command of royalist battalions at the crucial Battle of Cholet. At this battle several other women took part in the front lines, according to an aristocratic Vendean, Madame de la Rochejaquelein:

ravaged and massacred without mercy. I saw forty-two of my relatives perish successively; but the murder of my father, committed before my very eyes, filled me with rage and despair. From this moment on, I resolved to sacrifice my body to the King, to offer my soul to God, and I swore to fight until death or victory.[63]

Born in 1770 in the village of Soulaines, Bordereau's nickname *L'angevine* indicated that she was from the region of Anjou, at the northern limits of the Vendée. She was a rough, strong, fierce peasant woman who used swords, pistols, and her bare hands to slay dozens of her enemies in many major combats, including the Battles of Saint-Florent and Thouars. Her fame spread throughout the Vendean army, inspiring the men of her side to fight with greater courage and ardor. Madame de la Rochejaquelein gave a second description of Bordereau in her memoirs:

She was of ordinary height and very ugly. One day at Cholet, they pointed her out to me: "See that soldier who has sleeves of a color different from his coat. That's a girl who fights like a lion." She was named Renee Bordereau, called l'Angevine, and served in the cavalry. Her unbelievable courage was celebrated throughout the whole army.[64]

Bordereau committed many acts of mercy and compassion as well. When several of her fellow soldiers stole fifteen hundred francs from a local woman, she saw to it personally that the money was returned. She helped many families hide from the republicans and carried one paralyzed woman from one hiding place to the next. But she also found that she could not return to normal life after the Vendean revolt ended in 1796. A prominent symbol of the royalist cause, she was imprisoned for several years under the reign of Napoléon Bonaparte. When the monarchy was restored under Louis XVIII in 1814, she was freed and granted a pension by the king. After her release, she remained in Paris, enjoying the notoriety that came with her military exploits. Although she had never been to school and could not read or write, she dictated memoirs of her experiences in a short book, *Military Life in the Vendée*, that was published for the first time in 1814.

Returning to Civilian Life

Renee Bordereau's memoirs appeared at a time when France had again just experienced the troubles of war—this time under the rule of Napoléon, who conscripted millions of young Frenchmen and commanded a series of campaigns that saw French armies invading and occupying nearly every corner of the

The Uprising in Vendée

The aristocratic Madame de Sapinaud, in her *Historical Memoirs of the Vendée*, quoted in Winifred Stephens's *Women of the French Revolution*, describes the outbreak of the Vendée uprising, when peasants seeking a leader came to her husband:

The fighting began on March 12, 1793. The peasant rose up at La Bretiere. Then they spread to the neighborhood parishes and approached M. Sapinaud de Bois-Huguet who was better known as La Verrie. "We make you our general," they said. He told them, "My friends, this is an earthen pot against an iron pot, weak against strong. How much can we do, one department against eighty-two? We will be beaten. . . . But these honest peasants were far from accepting his reasons. . . .

The once so modest Charette could hardly be recognized: His violet clothes were embroidered with green silk and silver . . . and some pretty young women followed his entourage. . . . The rearguard was less glamorous: Many women from the quarters of poverty, most of them barefoot . . . in rags, as were their little children; their men had been killed, their huts burnt down. . . . They had no other refuge but the army.

European continent. Napoléon arrived when the many years of revolutionary bloodshed in France were making the people hungry for stability. In 1799 he took advantage of his renown as a military commander to overthrow the Directory and seize power as the sole ruler of France.

In the meantime, the women soldiers of France who had survived the Revolution made their best efforts to return to normal civilian life. Because they did not carry legal status as combatants, they could not benefit from the favors and money granted by France to its sick and wounded veterans. Instead, they had to petition for what they sought. One such petition from a female soldier read:

Citoyenne Felicite Duguet, called Va-de-bon-coeur, a native of Versailles in the department of Seine-et-Oise, declares that, the sacred love of country by which she is animated not allowing her to view the dangers that menaced it with indifference, she had disguised her sex and marched voluntarily in defense of the country; that she constantly accompanied the 1st battalion of the Nievre and shared in its labors and dangers; that she was seriously wounded; that under the law excluding women from the army she could no longer remain with the said battalion and so received a leave with certificates of honorable service; and that she then established her domicile in this department; for which reason she requests the administration to obtain the relief for her that is necessary and due.[65]

The Revolution had turned the life of Felicite Duguet upside down, as it had done for millions of Frenchwomen who found themselves living in a radically different nation at the end of the eighteenth century. The French Revolution would have long-lasting effects in the rest of the world as well. It would inspire republican revolutions throughout Europe in the nineteenth century, and it would motivate socialists fighting a revolution in twentieth-century Russia. Those seeking an end to monarchs and their tyranny took inspiration in the revolutionary ardor for equality and justice, while their opponents pointed out the Revolution's many horrors. The role played by women in this important event also provided inspiration to those seeking to raise women from their traditional, subservient role in public life.

Epilogue:
Liberty and Sorority, but Not Equality

Although many women had fought and died for the French Revolution, others had simply escaped. These émigrés found refuge in other European countries as well as in the United States. In America one such émigré, Madame de La Tour du Pin, found the simple republican virtues that had been advocated by the dandified writers and philosophers of the French salons. One American in particular drew Madame de La Tour du Pin's admiration:

> Mrs. Renslaer was a woman of thirty who spoke French well. . . . From the newspapers she had learned the state of the parties in France, the blunders which had caused the Revolution, the vices of the upper classes and the follies of the middle classes. With extraordinary insight, she had grasped the causes and effects of the disorders in our country better than we had ourselves.[66]

Eventually, Madame de La Tour du Pin would return to England and, after Napoléon's coup of 1799, to her homeland. Many others in her situation would return as well, although those remaining on an official list of émigrés still risked confiscation of their property and execution. Those who did return found a country where monarchy was dead and where the bitter memories of civil war among social classes were still dividing the citizens.

New Rights for Women

Yet the French Revolution did succeed in changing the lowly legal status of women. In 1791, when the National Assembly lifted guild restrictions, women gained the right to enter professions, such as publishing, that were previously open only to men. Women gained the right to inherit property by the law that ended primogeniture, the feudal custom of passing all property to the eldest son. By a divorce law of September 22, 1792, Frenchwomen also gained the right to demand a divorce. They gained the right to testify as witnesses in court and, in 1793, married women were granted the right to sign contracts on their own, without the required consent of their husbands.

There were many wider and significant effects outside of the laws. By ruthlessly suppressing the aristocracy, the Revolution threw open writing and arts to a new audience. Women authors of the revolutionary era found their voices, saw their words in print, and for the first time took part in political debate. In her book *The Other Enlightenment*, author Carla Hesse hails the "democratization" of culture brought about by the French Revolution:

> There was no "women's revolution" in 1789, but . . . the French Revolution opened up the unprecedented opportunity for women to participate in public political discourse and debate . . . [making] it possible for the first time in history for almost any woman or man to appeal publicly to the reason of fellow citizens and, ultimately, to win civil and political equality for women—even if it took more than a century to do so.[67]

Legally, however, women remained in a subsidiary role in French society. Their new rights did not include voting, holding public office, or bearing arms. The National Convention also rejected a proposal by Jean-Jacques-Regis de Cambaceres to make a wife's legal status fully equal to that of her husband. And in the wake of the Revolution, under the empire of Napoléon, Frenchwomen were again reduced to second-class citizens. Divorce was further restricted (and finally abolished altogether in 1816). Women lost the right to sell property or plead their case in court without their husband's consent. The Napoleonic Code, the set of laws dictated by the emperor, gave fathers sole authority over their minor children (by Article 373 and Article 148) and even forbade women from witnessing legal documents (by Article 37). By the copyright law of 1793, unmarried women and widows held full property rights in their written works. But within a marriage, written works remained community property. French husbands had to give permission for their wives to publish their works or sign any kind of business contract—a restriction that lasted until 1965.

In her essay "On Women Writers," Germaine de Staël deplored the generally sad state of affairs between the sexes:

> Ever since the Revolution men have deemed it politically and morally useful to reduce women to a state of the most absurd mediocrity. They have addressed women only in a wretched language with no more delicacy than wit. Women have no

longer any motive to develop their minds. . . . If Frenchmen could give their wives all the virtues of English-women, including retiring habits and a taste for solitude, they would do very well to prefer such virtues to the gifts of brilliant wit. All the French will manage to do this way, however, is to make their women read nothing, know nothing, and become incapable of carrying on a conversation with an interesting idea.[68]

For the rest of the world, the French Revolution served as an example of the best and worst aspects of political transformation. Its violence and fanaticism gave arguments for those holding to the status quo, while its notions of liberty and democracy have inspired those fighting for change. For women, Olympe de Gouges, Madame Roland, Renee Bordereau, and many other women of the Revolution provide examples of breaking away from society's limits and fighting—sometimes dying—for ideals. For all students of this event, women emerged as its most powerful symbols, whether they were idealized fighters for the republic and liberty, as in Marianne, or despised emblems of aristocratic corruption, such as Marie-Antoinette. Although they waited more than a century for "liberty, equality, and fraternity" with men, Frenchwomen have always had a wealth of heroines for inspiration in their struggle.

Notes

Introduction: Liberty, Equality, Sorority

1. Marilyn Yalom, *Blood Sisters: The French Revolution in Women's Memory.* New York: Basic, 1993, p. 8.
2. Quoted in Darline Gay Levy, Harriet Branson Applewhite, and Mary Durham Johnson, eds., *Women in Revolutionary Paris 1789–1795.* Urbana: University of Illinois Press, 1979, pp. 24–26.

Chapter 1: A World Overthrown: Women of the Aristocracy

3. Germaine de Staël, *Considerations sur la Revolution Francaise.* Paris: Talliender, 1983, p. 101.
4. Quoted in Yalom, *Blood Sisters*, p. 22.
5. Quoted in Jacques Levron, *Daily Life at Versailles in the Seventeenth and Eighteenth Centuries.* New York: Macmillan, 1968, p. 198.
6. Felice Harcourt, ed., *Memoirs of Madame de La Tour du Pin.* New York: McCall, 1971, pp. 26–27.
7. Quoted in Yalom, *Blood Sisters*, p. 39.
8. Quoted in Yalom, *Blood Sisters*, p. 49.

9. Stanley Loomis, *Paris in the Terror: June 1793–July 1794.* Philadelphia: J.B. Lippincott, 1964, p. 16.
10. Quoted in Loomis, *Paris in the Terror*, p. 137.
11. Quoted in Simon Schama, *Citizens: A Chronicle of the French Revolution.* New York: Alfred A. Knopf, 1989, p. 740.

Chapter 2: The Radical Urban Vanguard: Laborers and Market Women of Paris

12. David Garrioch, *The Making of Revolutionary Paris.* Berkeley and Los Angeles: University of California Press, 2002, p. 39.
13. Quoted in Harriet Applewhite and Darline G. Levy, "Women and Militant Citizenship in Revolutionary Paris," in Sara E. Melzer and Leslie W. Rabine, eds., *Rebel Daughters: Women and the French Revolution.* London: Oxford University Press, 1992, p. 83.
14. Schama, *Citizens*, pp. 462–63.
15. Quoted in Richard Cobb and Colin Jones, eds., *Voices of the French Revolution.* Topsfield, MA: Salem House, 1988, p. 190.

16. Quoted in Cobb and Jones, *Voices of the French Revolution*, p. 136.

17. George Rude, *The French Revolution: Its Causes, Its History, and Its Legacy After 200 Years*. New York: Weidenfeld & Nicolson, 1988, p. 89.

18. Quoted in Dominique Godineau, *The Women of Paris and Their French Revolution*. Berkeley and Los Angeles: University of California Press, 1998, p. 110.

19. Quoted in Cobb and Jones, *Voices of the French Revolution*, p. 156.

20. Quoted in Applewhite and Levy, "Women and Militant Citizenship in Revolutionary Paris," p. 96.

21. Quoted in Godineau, *The Women of Paris and Their French Revolution*, p. 179.

22. Quoted in Godineau, *The Women of Paris and Their French Revolution*, p. 335.

23. Quoted in Godineau, *The Women of Paris and Their French Revolution*, pp. 344–45.

Chapter 3: Women of the Societies

24. Jean Abray, "Feminism in the French Revolution," *American Historical Review*, February 1975, pp. 45–46.

25. Schama, *Citizens*, p. 530.

26. Quoted in Applewhite and Levy, "Women and Militant Citizenship in Revolutionary Paris," p. 88.

27. Joan B. Landes, *Women and the Public Sphere in the Age of the French Revolution*. Ithaca, NY: Cornell University Press, 1988, p. 141.

28. "Regulations of the Society of Revolutionary Republican Women," July 9, 1793, *Liberty, Equality, Fraternity: Exploring the French Revolution*. http://chnm.gmu.edu/revolution.

29. "Regulations of the Society of Revolutionary Republican Women."

30. Quoted in Levy, Applewhite, and Johnson, *Women in Revolutionary Paris 1789–1795*, pp. 169–70.

31. Quoted in Levy, Applewhite, and Johnson, *Women in Revolutionary Paris 1789–1795*, p. 170.

32. Quoted in Levy, Applewhite, and Johnson, *Women in Revolutionary Paris 1789–1795*, p. 200.

Chapter 4: Women Writers

33. Germaine de Staël, "On Women Writers," in Vivian Folkenflik, ed., *An Extraordinary Woman: Selected Writings of Germaine de Staël*. New York: Columbia University Press, 1987, p. 202.

34. Quoted in Vera Lee, *The Reign of Women in Eighteenth Century France*. Cambridge, MA:

Schenkman, 1975, pp. 76–77.

35. Winifred Stephens, *Women of the French Revolution*. New York: E.P. Dutton, 1922, p. 78.

36. Germaine de Staël, "The Opening of the Estates General May 1789," in Folkenflik, *An Extraordinary Woman*, pp. 363–64.

37. Carla Hesse, *The Other Enlightenment: How French Women Became Modern*. Princeton, NJ: Princeton University Press, 2001, p. 92.

38. Quoted in Hesse, *The Other Enlightenment*, p. 8.

39. Hesse, *The Other Enlightenment*, p. 25.

Chapter 5:
Peasants and Villagers

40. Gita May, *Madame Roland and the Age of Revolution*. New York: Columbia University Press, 1970, p. 147.

41. Schama, *Citizens*, p. 324.

42. Schama, *Citizens*, p. 430.

43. Quoted in Francine du Plessix Gray, *At Home with the Marquis de Sade: A Life*. New York: Penguin, 1999, p. 296.

44. Yalom, *Blood Sisters*, p. 197.

45. Quoted in Stephens, *Women of the French Revolution*, p. 253.

46. Olympe de Gouges, "Declaration of the Rights of Women," 1791, *Modern History Sourcebook*.

www.fordham.edu/halsall/mod/1791degouge1.html.

47. Quoted in "The Trial of Olympe de Gouges," *Liberty, Equality, Fraternity: Exploring the French Revolution*. http://chnm.gmu.edu/revolution.

48. Quoted in Melzer and Rabine, *Rebel Daughters*, p. 115.

Chapter 6:
Women and Religion

49. Mona Ozouf, "De-Christianization," in Francois Furet and Mona Ozouf, eds., Arthur Goldhammer, trans., *A Critical Dictionary of the French Revolution*, vol. 1. Cambridge, MA: Belknap Press of Harvard University Press, 1989, p. 22.

50. John McManners, *The French Revolution and the Church*. New York: Harper & Row, 1969, pp. 32–33.

51. McManners, *The French Revolution and the Church*, p. 35.

52. Loomis, *Paris in the Terror*, pp. 247–48.

53. Quoted in Gray, *At Home with the Marquis de Sade*, p. 339.

54. Stephens, *Women of the French Revolution*, p. 233.

55. Ozouf, "De-Christianization," p. 31.

Chapter 7: Women Soldiers

56. Quoted in David E. Jones, *Women Warriors: A History*. Washington, DC: Brassey's, 1997, p. 191.

57. Quoted in Levy, Applewhite, and Johnson, *Women in Revolutionary Paris 1789–1795*, pp. 72–73.

58. Alan Forrest, *The Soldiers of the French Revolution*. Durham, NC: Duke University Press, 1990, pp. 149–50.

59. Stephens, *Women of the French Revolution*, p. 182.

60. Quoted in Levy, Applewhite, and Johnson, *Women in Revolutionary Paris 1789–1795*, pp. 225–26.

61. Quoted in Schama, *Citizens*, p. 694.

62. Quoted in Jones, *Women Warriors*, p. 191.

63. Quoted in Yalom, *Blood Sisters*, p. 199.

64. Quoted in Yalom, *Blood Sisters*, p. 201.

65. Quoted in Jean-Paul Bertaud, *The Army of the French Revolution: From Citizen-Soldiers to Instrument of Power*. Princeton, NJ: Princeton University Press, 1988, pp. 53–54.

Epilogue: Liberty and Sorority, but Not Equality

66. Harcourt, *Memoirs of Madame de La Tour du Pin*, p. 239.

67. Hesse, *The Other Enlightenment*, p. 55.

68. Staël, "On Women Writers," p. 203.

Chronology

1789

May 5 The Estates General, representatives of the clergy (First Estate), nobility (Second), and bourgeoisie (Third), begins meeting in Versailles to deal with the economic crisis in France.

June 20 Three days after declaring the founding of a National Assembly, members of the Third Estate swear to write a new constitution. On July 9 they will rename themselves the Constituent Assembly.

July 14 In search of arms, citizens of Paris storm the Bastille prison in Paris, kill its governor, and free seven prisoners.

August 4 Members of the Second Estate declare the surrender of their feudal rights and titles.

August 26 The Assembly promulgates the Declaration of the Rights of Man and of the Citizen.

October 5 A crowd of Parisian women march to the king's palace at Versailles to demand bread and the king's return to Paris.

November 2 The Assembly nationalizes church property. The value of land seized from the church will back up a new currency known as the assignat.

1790

January A political club begins meeting at the Jacobin monastery in Paris. The Jacobins will emerge as a powerful and radical revolutionary faction.

May 21 The government of Paris, known as the Commune, reorganizes the city into forty-eight sections.

July 14 The king accepts a new constitution written by the Assembly.

October 31 The legislature abolishes all trade barriers within France.

1791

March 2 Traditional trade guilds are abolished.

June 20 The king and his family flee Paris for safe haven in Austrian-controlled territory. They will be intercepted at Varennes and returned to Paris.

July 17 Under General de Lafayette, a detachment of the National Guard opens fire on a protesting crowd on the Champ de Mars in Paris.

September 30 The National Assembly completes a new constitution, then is dissolved and replaced by the Legislative Assembly.

1792

March The Girondin faction of moderate representatives forms a government ministry.

April 20 France declares war on Austria and Germany.

July 25 By the Brunswick Manifesto, Prussia, Austria, and other European states declare war on revolutionary France.

August 10 Parisians storm the Tuileries palace and remove the king and queen to the Temple prison.

September 2 Rumors of an invasion by Austrian troops provoke a massacre of prisoners in Paris.

September 21 A National Convention begins meeting and officially abolishes the French monarchy.

1793

January 21 King Louis XVI is executed in Paris.

March An uprising against the revolutionary government begins in the Vendée region.

April 6 The Convention forms a Committee of Public Safety to try and condemn enemies of the Revolution.

June 2 Girondist deputies are banished from the National Convention and placed under arrest by their rivals in the Jacobin faction.

June 24 The Convention promulgates the Constitution of 1793.

July 13 Charlotte Corday assassinates Jean-Paul Marat.

October 16 Queen Marie-Antoinette is executed.

October 30 Women's revolutionary societies are banned by the Convention.

November 10 The Assembly decrees the abolition of Christian worship and replaces it with the national Cult of Reason.

1794

March 13 Leaders of the Cordeliers club are arrested and condemned to be executed.

March 29 Georges-Jacques Danton is arrested and condemned to death.

July 27 Maximilien Robespierre is swept from power as head of the Committee of Public Safety.

November The Convention closes the Jacobin club.

Women of the French Revolution

1795

April Bread shortages lead to riots in Paris. The Convention declares a state of siege and arrests radical deputies.

August 22 The National Convention passes the Constitution of 1795, which will be ratified on September 23.

October 5 An artillery detachment under Napoléon Bonaparte disperses a crowd of protesters with a "whiff of grapeshot."

October 26 The National Convention is dissolved and a five-member Directory takes power.

For Further Reading

Books

Crane Brinton, *The Anatomy of Revolution.* New York: Vintage, 1965. The author courageously attempts to summarize the English, American, French, and Russian revolutions and find common threads in all of them. He concludes that in many cases revolution brings little change to the lives of ordinary people but instead represents merely a transfer of power from one privileged class of politicians to the next.

William Doyle, *The French Revolution: A Very Short Introduction.* New York: Oxford University Press, 2001. A concise treatment of the Revolution for those just beginning study of this event. The author gives background information on the French monarchy and gives his opinion on the Revolution's long-lasting effects on French and world history. The book also provides a timeline, a list of further reading, and the revolutionary calendar.

Christopher Hibbert, *The Days of the French Revolution.* New York: Perennial, 1999. An introduction to the history of the French Revolution for the general reader who is studying the period for the first time. The book includes maps, a glossary, and a chronology, as well as twenty-eight pages of black-and-white illustrations.

Joe H. Kirchberger, *The French Revolution and Napoleon: An Eyewitness History.* New York: Facts On File, 1989. Provides detailed background on the Revolution and the Napoleonic era that followed. The book includes a large collection of primary-source material from the era, including letters, diaries, newspapers, journals, and speeches.

Don Nardo, ed., *The French Revolution.* San Diego: Greenhaven, 1999. The editor uses contemporary documents and writings to describe the causes of the Revolution, significant events, social and cultural aspects of the Revolution, and the impact of the Revolution on the rest of the world.

Steven Otfinoski, *Triumph and Terror: The French Revolution.* New York: Facts On File, 1993. An overview of the causes, events, and impacts of the French Revolution for young adult readers.

Web Sites

Freedom or Death: A Provocative Exploration of the French Revolution
(http://library.thinkquest.org/C0062 57/default.shtml). A ThinkQuest site designed by and for history students. Contains biographies of leading figures of the Revolution, a multimedia section with music and a video, a timeline, and sidebars exploring various cultural aspects and little-known events of the Revolution.

French Revolution Links Page
(http://userweb.port.ac.uk/~andressd /frlinks.htm). A guide to Web pages concerning the French Revolution, maintained by David Andress, a lecturer at the University of Portsmouth. The links direct students to articles, lectures, and essays, in English as well as French.

Liberty, Equality, Fraternity: Exploring the French Revolution
(http://chnm.gmu.edu/revolution). A guided illustrated tour through the French Revolution, with 350 text documents as well as maps, songs, and illustrations from the period. Includes twelve topical essays as well as a timeline and glossary.

Modern History Sourcebook (www. fordham.edu/halsall/mod/mods book.html). A vast and incredibly useful collection of documents from all periods and places. Includes several dozen descriptions and primary-source documents, including letters, speeches, and proclamations, translated and indexed, from the French Revolution.

Works Consulted

Books

Jean-Paul Bertaud, *The Army of the French Revolution: From Citizen-Soldiers to Instrument of Power.* Princeton, NJ: Princeton University Press, 1988. The author describes the revolutionary armies from a political and social standpoint, giving interesting detail on everyday life for common soldiers, as well as the maneuvering of politicians seeking to control and wield a new kind of military force.

Richard Cobb and Colin Jones, eds., *Voices of the French Revolution.* Topsfield, MA: Salem House, 1988. An illustrated collection of documents of all kinds—speeches, newspaper articles, pamphlets, and decrees—from the French Revolution, providing a view of the fanaticism of revolutionary leaders and the great enthusiasm, as well as hatred, they stirred up in people of all classes.

Vivian Folkenflik, ed., *An Extraordinary Woman: Selected Writings of Germaine de Staël.* New York: Columbia University Press, 1987. A collection of essays by Germaine de Staël, a witness to the Revolution who writes with great insight about many aspects of French society, particularly the role of women.

Alan Forrest, *The Soldiers of the French Revolution.* Durham, NC: Duke University Press, 1990. A description of the daily lives and struggles of the men, and in a few cases women, who took up arms to defend the Revolution.

Francois Furet and Mona Ozouf, eds., Arthur Goldhammer, trans. *A Critical Dictionary of the French Revolution.* Cambridge, MA: Belknap Press of Harvard University Press, 1989. Scholarly essays by leading modern historians of the revolutionary period, grouped into Events, Actors, Institutions and Creations, Ideas, Historians, and Commentators. This exceptionally informative and insightful collection is the most useful single volume on this event for researchers.

David Garrioch, *The Making of Revolutionary Paris.* Berkeley and Los Angeles: University of California Press, 2002. The author uncovers the lives of ordinary Parisians through the eighteenth century and explains how the capital's stark social divisions played an important role in the chaotic unfolding of the French Revolution.

Dominique Godineau, *The Women of Paris and Their French Revolution.* Berkeley and Los Angeles: University of California Press, 1998. A long and very detailed survey of the Revolution as experienced and carried out by the women of the French capital. The author focuses on the issues most directly affecting women, including bread riots, female political clubs, conflicts such as the "War of the Cockades," the fight over prices and supply in the public marketplaces, and the uprising of May 1795, which resulted in the total ban on political activity by women.

Francine du Plessix Gray, *At Home with the Marquis de Sade: A Life.* New York: Penguin, 1999. An account of the chaotic personal life of the decadent writer, focusing on the women in his life and detailing the hedonism and the horrors of France under the monarchy and during the Revolution.

Felice Harcourt, ed., *Memoirs of Madame de La Tour du Pin.* New York: McCall, 1971. The aristocratic émigré describes her life before the Revolution, when she moved in the highest circles of the French nobility, as well as her flight from revolutionary France and her new life as a refugee in the United States.

Carla Hesse, *The Other Enlightenment: How French Women Became Modern.* Princeton, NJ: Princeton University Press, 2001. During the Revolution female writers were freed of most legal restrictions on what they could write and how they could publish their works. This book gives detailed histories of the women writers of the Revolution and follows the progress, and faltering, of women's literary rights in the postrevolutionary period.

David E. Jones, *Women Warriors: A History.* Washington, DC: Brassey's, 1997. Examines female soldiers and military leaders from different parts of the world, from Asia to Europe and North America, from myth and from reality, revealing that their courage and skill often equaled that of men.

Alex Karmel, *Guillotine in the Wings: A New Look at the French Revolution and Its Relevance to America Today.* New York: McGraw-Hill, 1972. The author speculates on the possibility of a violent revolution in the United States, comparing the social tensions of modern America with France under the Bourbon monarchy.

Joan B. Landes, *Women and the Public Sphere in the Age of the French Revolu-*

tion. Ithaca, NY: Cornell University Press, 1988. The author describes the fall of the French monarchy as the birth of modern feminism. She argues that the "bourgeois" government and society that followed the Revolution silenced women in the public sphere, relegated them to domestic life, and imposed gender roles that inspired the nineteenth-century drive for women's rights and suffrage.

Vera Lee, *The Reign of Women in Eighteenth Century France.* Cambridge, MA: Schenkman, 1975. An objective description of women of all social levels in prerevolutionary France, covering their education, family roles, legal rights, and work experiences. The book points out that women in general had greater influence and power before the Revolution, when their expected roles were clearly defined, than after it, when they were relegated to the background as second-class citizens of the new republic.

Jacques Levron, *Daily Life at Versailles in the Seventeenth and Eighteenth Centuries.* New York: Macmillan, 1968. An examination of the intricate workings of the royal court at Versailles and how it changed in the years leading up to the Revolution.

Darline Gay Levy, Harriet Branson Applewhite, and Mary Durham Johnson, eds., *Women in Revolutionary Paris 1789–1795.* Urbana: University of Illinois Press, 1979. A collection of original documents, reports, speeches, and letters from women of the revolutionary period, testifying to the significant events of their times and providing fascinating details on the excitement, violence, and despair brought to their daily lives.

Stanley Loomis, *Paris in the Terror: June 1793–July 1794.* Philadelphia: J.B. Lippincott, 1964. A lively account of the leading figures of the Revolution, including Charlotte Corday, Danton, and Robespierre.

Gita May, *Madame Roland and the Age of Revolution.* New York: Columbia University Press, 1970. Background and description of the turmoil among French revolutionary leaders, in particular the Girondin circle surrounding Madame Roland and her husband.

Arno J. Mayer, *The Furies: Violence and Terror in the French and Russian Revolutions.* Princeton, NJ: Princeton University Press, 2000. The author seeks common causes for the violence and fanaticism unleashed by the two most significant revolutions of modern times.

John McManners, *The French Revolution and the Church.* New York: Harper &

Row, 1969. A scholarly treatise on the tangled history of the Catholic Church during the French Revolution.

Sara E. Melzer and Leslie W. Rabine eds., *Rebel Daughters: Women and the French Revolution.* London: Oxford University Press, 1992. A collection of fourteen essays on women and the ideology and politics of the Revolution, also covering the permanent effects of the Revolution on women in French society and culture.

Karen Offen, *European Feminisms, 1750–1950: A Political History.* Stanford, CA: Stanford University Press, 2000. The author discusses the effects of local languages, religion, culture, and government on the drive for women's social and political rights.

George Rude, *The French Revolution: Its Causes, Its History, and Its Legacy After 200 Years.* New York: Weidenfeld & Nicolson, 1988. An author who specializes in the history of the French Revolution gives his summary of the events and his opinion on the underlying causes of the Revolution and the violence it brought.

Simon Schama, *Citizens: A Chronicle of the French Revolution.* New York: Knopf, 1989. A well-written, detailed, and absorbing account of the French Revolution. The book describes in detail the financial crisis that sparked the Revolution; debunks the popular myths surrounding its most famous events, such as the fall of the Bastille; and gives in-depth prose portraits of the Revolution's leaders. It includes more than two hundred contemporary images and artworks that illustrate the main events and participants.

Germaine de Staël, *Considerations sur la Revolution Francaise.* Paris: Talliender, 1983. Madame de Staël was the daughter of Jacques Necker and an eyewitness to the French Revolution. This book of personal essays, written a few years after the event, offers brilliant insights into the motives of the Revolution's most important figures as well as social and cultural tensions and tendencies that contributed to the Revolution's fanaticism and violence.

Winifred Stephens, *Women of the French Revolution.* New York: E.P. Dutton, 1922. A book of anecdotes describing women of all social classes and occupations during the Revolution. Although the writing is pretentious and the information outdated, the book offers details of the lives of ordinary and well-known women of the period that are interesting to the researcher.

Alexis de Tocqueville, *The Old Regime and the French Revolution.* New York:

Anchor, 1955. Better known for his tour through the United States that resulted in *Democracy in America*, Tocqueville had a firsthand knowledge of France as a native of that country and keen insight into the social and political circumstances that brought about the French Revolution. In this book he gives an account of the causes and consequences of the Revolution up to his own time, the middle of the nineteenth century, and demonstrates how the Revolution resulted from political currents under way in France well before 1789.

Marilyn Yalom, *Blood Sisters: The French Revolution in Women's Memory.* New York: Basic Books, 1993. A book describing the written memoirs left by women of all social classes during the Revolution. The author covers relatives and ladies-in-waiting of Queen Marie-Antoinette; Madame Roland and her experiences as the wife of a committed revolutionary before she went to the guillotine; the wife of Maximilien Robespierre; Germaine de Staël; peasant women and fighters of the Vendée; the émigré Madame de La Tour du Pin; and several others.

Periodical

Jean Abraya "Feminism in the French Revolution," *American Historical Review*, February 1975.

Internet Sources

Olympe de Gouges, "Declaration of the Rights of Women," 1791, *Modern History Sourcebook*. www.fordham.edu/halsall/mod/1791degouge1.html.

"Regulations of the Society of Revolutionary Republican Women," July 9, 1793, *Liberty, Equality, Fraternity: Exploring the French Revolution*. http://chnm.gmu.edu/revolution.

"The Trial of Olympe de Gouges," *Liberty, Equality, Fraternity: Exploring the French Revolution*. http://chnm.gmu.edu/revolution.

Index

Abbaye prison, 64
Abray, Jean, 44
Adelaide (Keralio), 63
Allure, de Verte, 57
Alsace, 95
Amar, Andre, 37
Amazons, 30, 63, 92
Amis de la Loi, Les (Friends of the Law), 74
Ancien Regime (Old Regime), 6–8, 55
Angers, 84
Anjou, 101
aristocrats
  condemnation of, 18
  as landowners, 8, 12
  literary interest of, 58
  population of, 12
  as refugees, 72–73
  riots and, 30
  taxes and, 8
  woman's rights and, 12–14
Arras, 62–63
assignat, 40
Aubry, Mademoiselle, 87
Austria
  Marie-Antoinette and, 15, 35
  royal family's attempted escape to, 18–19
  September massacres and, 21–22

Babaroux, Charles, 25
Bardot, Brigitte, 36
Barre, Cordule, 91
Basancon, 71
Bastille
  fall of, 11, 26, 29, 74
  Festival of the Federation and, 17–18
Beaubourg, 34

Beaumont, Mme. de, 20
Bedford, Lord, 51
Belgium, 90
Benedict XV, 91
Blood Sisters (Yalom), 31, 62
Bologna, 88
Bonaparte, Napoléon
  abolition of new calendar by, 75
  coup of 1799 and, 60, 101–102
  see also Napoleonic Code
Bordereau, Renee, 100–101
Bouche de Fer (Mouth of Iron) (newspaper), 44
Bourbon kings, 92
bourgeoisie. *See* middle class
Brissot, Jacques Pierre, 47
Brittany, 73, 77

cahiers de doleances (complaint books), 8–9
Cambaceres, Jean-Jacques-Regis de, 105
Campan, Jeanne-Louise, 19–20
Casta, Laeticia, 36
Castel St. Angelo, 88
Cercle Social, 44
Champ de Mars, 19, 33
Chatelet quarter, 29
Chaumette, Anaxagore, 77
Cholet, battle of, 100–101
Christianity. *See* religion
Church of Le May-sur-Evre, 79
Church of Sainte Marguerite, 29
Citizeness Aubry, 87
Civil Constitution of the Clergy, 83, 88
clergy/priest
  forced marriages and, 85
  new constitutional, 78, 83
  refractory, 78–79, 83–84, 88

as refugees, 73
roles of, 80
taxes and, 8
clubs, 38, 42–44, 74
Cobb, Richard, 26
cockades, 18, 35, 37, 50, 78
Committee of Public Safety, 11, 85, 88–89, 97
Commune of Pads, 25
Compiegne, 89
Conciergerie prison, 25, 62
Condorcet, Marquis de, 44, 47
Confederation of the Friends of Truth), 43–44
Considerations (Staël), 13, 20, 60
Constitution of 1791, 32–33
convents
closure of, 82
in Mons, 90
religious education and, 83–84, 89
Sacred Heart, 87
see also nuns; religion
Corday, Charlotte, 22–25, 64
Cordeliers, 44, 49, 74
counterrevolutionaries
attacks on, 32–33
Jacobin supporters and, 40
petition to punish, 46
September massacres and, 35
Society of Revolutionary Republican
Women and, 48–50
Crimes des Reines de France, Les (Crimes of the
Queen of France, The) (Keralio), 63–64

d'Aelders, Etta Palm, 43–45
Dansard, Claude, 44
Danton, Georges-Jacques, 66, 85
Dauphin, 88
"De-Christianization" (Ozouf), 81
Declaration of the Rights of Genius, 58
Declaration of the Rights of Man and of the
Citizen, 30, 46, 57
Declaration of the Rights of Women and the
Female Citizen, 50, 61, 76–77

de Gouges, Olympe
armed women bodyguards and, 94
execution of, 77
female suffrage and, 45
name origin of, 75
Deneuve, Catherine, 36
Dillon, Henriette-Lucy, 17
Directory, 60, 79, 102
Dordogne, 87
Doulon, 98–99
Dubois, Elizabeth Francois, 97–98
Duchesne, Rose Philippine, 87
Duguet, Citoyenne Felicite, 102–103
Dumouriez, Charles, 96–97
Dupont, Manette, 95

economy
assignat decline and, 40
food shortages and, 38–40
postwar bankruptcy and, 8
price controls and, 40, 49–50
raw material shortages and, 39–40
unemployment and, 39
Eglantine, Phillip Fabre d', 75
émigrés
condemnation of, 18
French informants and, 98
return of, 104
England, 63
Enlightenment, 7, 80, 95
Estates General
divisions of, 8
grievances and, 9–10
National Assembly and, 10, 30
reform and, 12, 17
European Feminism (Offen), 95
Evrard, Simonne, 23

Faubourg Saint-Antoine, 29, 33
Favre, Pierre Louis, 97–98
"Feminism in the French Revolution" (Abray), 44
Feraud, Jean, 41

Fernig, Felicite de, 95–97
Fernig, Louis Joseph de, 95–97
Fernig, Theophile de, 95–97
Fernig Regiment, 95
Festival of the Federation, 17–18, 84, 94
feudal system, 11, 72
Forrest, Alan, 94
Franz I, 15
Fraternal Society of Patriots of Both Sexes, 44
French Academy, 14
French Revolution and the Church, The (McManners), 82–83

Garrioch, David, 27
Gazette des Halles, La (newspaper), 57
Gely, Louise, 84–85
Germany, 89
Geunard, Elisabeth, 31
Gironde, 22
Girondins, 22–23, 40–41, 47–48
Goddess of Reason, 87
Gorsas, A.J., 49
Gouze, Marie. *See* de Gouges, Olympe
Great Fear, 71
Gregorian calendar, 75, 83
Grenoble, 87
Guinee, Anne Felicite, 39
Gynographs (la Bretonne), 52

Hesse, Carla, 63, 67, 105
Hotel de Ville, 29–30, 58
Hotel-Dieu, 82

Ile de la Cité, 82
insulteuses, 25–26
Italy, 89

Jacobins
  de-Christianization and, 77, 85–87
  formation of, 42
  Girondins and, 22–23
  women members of, 43
Jones, Colin, 26

Journal de l'Etat et du Citoyen (newspaper), 63
Jouy, 71

Keralio, Louise de
  cockade and, 78
  Le Mercure Nationale and, 57
  literary works of, 63–64
  parents of, 62
Kerenavent, Abbe, 85

la Bretonne, Restif de, 52
Labrousse, Suzette, 87–88
Lacombe, Claire, 46–47, 52, 54
ladies-in-waiting, 15–16, 21
Ladies of Mercy, 87
Lafayette, Marquis de, 30, 33, 78
la Fressange, Ines de, 36
"La Guerison de Marianne" (song), 36
Lamballe, Marie-Therese de, 21
L'Ami du Peuple (newspaper), 23
Landes, Joan, 47
L'angevine. See Bordereau, Renee
La Providence, 84
la Rochefoucault, Mademoiselle de, 99–100
la Rochejaquelein, Madame de, 73, 100–101
La Tour du Pin, Madame de, 17, 104
Law of Ventose, 91
Leclerc, Theophile, 54
Legislative Assembly, 46, 49–50, 52
Leon, Pauline, 44, 46–47, 54, 92–94
Les Halles, 28–29, 37
Les lettres bougrement patriotiques de la Mere Duchesne (newspaper), 33
L'Etoile du Matin (newspaper), 57
Levabre, Guillaume, 36
liberty cap, 36–37, 53, 70
"liberty, equality, and sorority," 11
Liberty, Equality, Fraternity (Web site), 39
Liege, 98
Longwy, 95
Loomis, Stanley, 22, 84
Louis XV, 17
Louis XVI

ban on clubs and, 42
Estates General and, 17
execution of, 25–26
flight of, from Paris, 18–19, 32
imprisonment of, 11
liberty cap and, 70
minister of finances and, 10
public opinion of, 15, 35
Louis XVIII, 101
Loustalot, Elysee, 29
Lyon, 64

Maastricht, 98
Mairie, 39
Maison-Dieu, 82
Making of Revolutionary Paris, The (Garrioch), 27
Marat, Jean-Paul, 23, 66
Marcourt, 73
Marianne, 36, 41, 70
Marie-Antoinette
  defiance of, 15–16
  execution of, 25–26
  flight of, from Paris, 18–19, 32
  Keralio's depiction of, 64
  resentment toward, 17
  spy accusations against, 15, 35
  as Widow Capet, 25
Marie-Therese, 15
market women
  female political societies and, 37–38, 53–54
  Jacobins and, 37
marriage, *Ancien Regime* and, 6
Massif Central, 77
McManners, John, 82, 84
Memoirs (Dillon), 17
Menerville, Madame de, 15
Mercier, Louis-Sebastien, 58
Mercure Nationale, Le (newspaper), 57, 63
Mere Duchesne (newspaper), 92
middle class, 6, 73, 80, 84
Military Life in the Vendée (Bordereau), 101
Mirabeau, 88

Modern History Sourcebook (Web site), 61, 97
monarchy
  absolute, 6
  Jacobins attack on, 77
  peasantry loyalty to, 77, 79
  petition to abolish, 47
  shortcomings of, 9
Monnet, Marie-Victoire, 71
Montagnards, 41, 47–48
Montbarey, Prince de, 16
Montmorin, Mme. de, 20
Montreuil, Renee-Pelagie de, 73

Napoleonic Code, 105
National Assembly
  church laws and, 82
  Estates General and, 10
  guild restrictions and, 104
  Jacobins and, 42
  "Ladies Request" and, 95
  riots and, 30, 33
  woman's right to bear arms and, 92–94
  see also National Convention
National Convention
  adoption of new calendar by, 75, 83–84
  banning of women from, 41
  ban on women in the army and, 97
  ban on women's clubs and, 37–38, 53–54
  cockade decree and, 35, 37
  de-Christianization decree and, 85–87
  Girondins and, 23, 47–49
  Jacobins control of, 37, 40
  repression of 1795 and, 40–41
  see also National Assembly
National Guard, 30, 33, 50, 94–96
Necker, Jacques, 10–11, 13, 58, 81
Necker, Madame, 13, 58
nobility, of the sword, 22
Notre Dame, 82, 86–87
nuns
  brutality against, 85
  Carmelite order, 89
  as émigrés, 90

execution of, 89–91
vows of, 81–82
see also convents; religion

Offen, Karen, 95
"On Women Writers" (Staël), 105
"Opening of the Estates General, The" (Staël), 20
Opera of Paris, 87
Order of Hospitaliers, 82
Order of St. Ursula, 89–90
Other Enlightenment, The (Hesse), 105
Ozouf, Mona, 81, 91

Paillot, Marie Clotilde, 90–91
Palais Royale, 43
Paris, 27–28
peasants
church and, 72, 77–80, 84
grain seizures and, 69, 71
hardships of, 8, 68–69
poaching and, 69
population of, 68
refugees and, 72–73
taxation of, 69
poisardes (fishwives), 28–29
primogeniture, 104
Prison de la Force, 21–22
privilege d'auteur, 55, 63
Provence, 77
Prussia, 21

Reign of Terror, 11, 25, 62, 88–89
religion
Catholic Church wealth and, 80
cults/seers, 87
de-Christianization and, 77, 85–87, 91
monasteries and, 82, 91
monks and, 82
pope and, 80, 83, 85
Protestant Reformation and, 80
revolutionary calendar and, 83–84
see also clergy/priest; convents; nuns

Revolutionary Committee, 39
riots
bread, 17, 29–32
Constitution of 1791 and, 32–33
food, 38–39, 40–41
grain, 71
petition for abolition of monarchy and, 33, 47
sugar, 33–35
Robert, Francois, 63
Robespierre, Augustine, 62
Robespierre, Charlotte, 62
Robespierre, Maximilien
de-Christianization and, 85
execution of, 62, 89
women bodyguards and, 94
Roland, Madame, 64–69
Roland, Monsieur, 64, 66–67
Rome, 80
Rousseau, Jean-Jacques, 7, 42–43
Roussel, Pierre, 50–51
Rude, George, 34
Rue Bouloy, 74
Rue Contrescarpe, 88
Rue de Grenelle, 46
Rue du Faubourg, 34–35
Rue Montorgueil, 38
Rue Saint Honore, 42, 47

Sade, Marquis de, 73, 85
Saint Florent, battle of, 101
Saint Marcel church, 35
Salic law, 14
salut de la patrie (nation's condition), 29–30
sansculottes, 19, 22, 25, 75
sans-culottides, 75
Schama, Simon, 30, 44, 69, 71
Seine-et-Oise, 102
Seine River, 28, 40, 46, 82
September massacres, 21–22, 35, 59–60
Seven Years War, 95
Social Contract, The (Rousseau), 8

Societe des Citoyennes Republicaines Revolutionnaires. *See* Society of Revolutionary Republican Women

Society of Revolutionary Republican Women
Article V of, 50
banning of, 38, 53
Jacobins and, 37, 49–50
price controls and, 49
regulations of, 49–50
uniforms of, 47

Soldier of the French Revolution, The (Forrest), 94

Souvenirs d'emigration (Menerville), 15

Staël, Germaine de
on affairs between sexes, 105–106
deportation of, 60
monarchy and, 59
as *salonniere*, 58–60
on women's literary works, 55, 57
on women's roles, 13

Stephens, Winifred, 88, 96

Supreme Reason, 86

Tableau de Paris (Mercier), 58

taxes
attempts to reform, 10–11
church and, 8, 80
imposing, on the rich, 50
poll, 33
tax farming and, 14

Temple of Reason. *See* Notre Dame

Temple Prison, 21, 25

Theot, Catherine, 88

Theroigne de Mericourt, Anne-Joseph, 30, 43–44, 73–75

Thouars, battle of, 101

Tirlemont, 98

Tour du Pin, Madame de, 104

Tourzel, Louise Elizabeth de, 18, 22

tricoteuses, 26

Tuileries palace, 17, 19, 32, 35

Ursulines, 84

Va-de-bon-coeur. *See* Duguet, Citoyenne Felicite

Vadier, Marc Guillaume, 88

Valenciennes, 89–91

Varennes, 19

Vendée uprising, 79, 98–102

Versailles
Estates General and, 20
Marie-Antoinette and, 15–16
royal family's flight from, 17–18, 32

Viroflay, 71

Visitation, 84

Voices of the French Revolution (Cobb and Jones), 26

War of the Cockades, 35, 37

Williams, Helen Maria, 26

Women in Revolutionary Paris 1789–1795 (d'Aelders), 45, 49

women soldiers
ban on, 97
as bodyguards, 94
disguised as men, 94
prostitutes and, 94–95
veteran benefits and, 102–103

women's rights
to bear arms, 33, 92–94, 105
to inherit property, 104
as passive citizens, 33, 46
publishing, 55, 57–58, 104
after revolution, 104–105

women writers
newspapers/pamphlets and, 11, 57
pamphleteers and, 15, 63
publishing rights of, 55, 57–58, 104
salonnieres and, 14, 20, 57
salons and, 14, 57–58, 74
as voices of the revolution, 57
see also Staël, Germaine de

Yalom, Marilyn, 8, 31, 62, 73

Picture Credits

❦

About the Author

❦

Thomas Streissguth has written more than fifty books of nonfiction for young readers since 1991. His Gale titles include *Understanding Beowulf*, *The Black Death*, *Life in Communist Russia*, *Life Among the Vikings*, and *History's Great Defeats: The Napoleonic Wars*. A music performance major and graduate of Yale University, he has worked as a teacher, journalist, and editor and has traveled to Europe, the Middle East, North Africa, Latin America, and Asia. He currently resides in Florida.

For Reference

Not to be taken from this room